Communication
and
Information
Technologies

Freedom of Choice for Latin America?

COMMUNICATION AND INFORMATION SCIENCE

A series of monographs, treatises, and texts
Edited by
MELVIN J. VOIGT
University of California, San Diego

Recent Titles:

Alan Baughcum and Gerald Faulhaber • Telecommunications Access and Public Policy
Mary Cassata and Thomas Skill • Life on Daytime Television
Herbert Dordick, Helen Bradley, & Burt Nanus • The Emerging Network Marketplace
William Dutton & Kenneth Kraemer • Modeling as Negotiating
Glen Fisher • American Communication in a Global Society
Oscar Gandy, Jr., Paul Espinosa, & Janusz Ordover • Proceedings from the Tenth Annual
    Telecommunications Policy Research Conference
Edmund Glenn • Man and Mankind: Conflict and Communication Between Cultures
Gerald Goldhaber, Harry Dennis III, Gary Richetto, & Osmo Wiio • Information Strategies
Bradley Greenberg, Michael Burgoon, Judee Burgoon, & Felipe Korzenny • Mexican Americans and
    the Mass Media
Heather Hudson • When Telephones Reach the Village
Robert Landau, James Bair, & Jean Siegman • Emerging Office Systems
James Larson • Television's Window on the World
John Lawrence • The Electronic Scholar
Armand Mattelart and Hector Schmucler • Communication and Information Technologies
Robert Meadow • Politics as Communication
Vincent Mosco • Broadcasting in the United States
Vincent Mosco • Policy Research in Telecommunications: Proceedings from the Eleventh Annual
    Telecommunications Policy Research Conference
Vincent Mosco • Pushbutton Fantasies
Kaarle Nordenstreng • The Mass Media Declaration of UNESCO
Kaarle Nordenstreng & Herbert Schiller • National Sovereignty and International Communication
Harry Otway & Malcolm Peltu • New Office Technology
Everett Rogers & Francis Balle • The Media Revolution in America and in Western Europe
Dan Schiller • Telematics and Government
Herbert Schiller • Information and the Crisis Economy
Herbert Schiller • Who Knows: Information in the Age of the Fortune 500
Jorge Schnitman • Film Industries in Latin America
Indu Singh • Telecommunications in the Year 2000
Jennifer Daryl Slack • Communication Technologies and Society
Keith Stamm • Newspaper Use and Community Ties
Sari Thomas • Studies in Mass Media and Technology, Volumes 1-3
Barry Truax • Acoustic Communication
Georgette Wang and Wimal Dissanayake • Continuity and Change in Communication Systems

In Preparation:

Sara Douglas • Labor's New Voice: Unions and the Mass Media
Fred Fejes • Imperialism, Media, and the Good Neighbor
Howard Fredericks • Cuban-American Radio Wars
W. J. Howell, Jr. • World Broadcasting in the Age of the Satellite
Kenneth Mackenzie • Organizational Design
David Paletz • Political Communication Research
Lea Stewart & Stella Ting-Toomey • Communication, Gender, and Sex Roles in Diverse Interaction
    Contexts
Robert Taylor • Value-Added Processes in Information Systems
Tran Van Dinh • Communication and Diplomacy in a Changing World
Tran Van Dinh • Independence, Liberation, Revolution
Frank Webster & Kevin Robins • Information Technology: A Luddite Analysis

Communication and Information Technologies:

Freedom of Choice for Latin America?

Armand Mattelart
University of Paris VIII

Hector Schmucler
Metropolitan Autonomous University, Mexico

Translated from the French by David Buxton

ABLEX PUBLISHING CORPORATION
NORWOOD, NEW JERSEY

Library of Congress Cataloging in Publication Data

Mattelart, Armand.
   Communication and information technologies.

   Translation of: L'ordinateur et le Tiers monde.
   Includes bibliographical references and index.
   1. Computer industry—Latin America. 2. Computer
industry—Developing countries. 3. Computers—Social
aspects—Latin America. 4. Computers—Social aspects—
Developing countries. I. Schmucler, Hector. II. Title.
HD9696.C63L38513 1985   338.4'700164'098   85–1348
ISBN 0–89391–214–X

Ablex Publishing Corporation
355 Chestnut Street
Norwood, New Jersey 07648

Contents

Tables

Figures

Acknowledgments

This study would not have been possible were it not for the economic assistance of the International Development Research Center in Canada. We are especially indebted to Elizabeth Fox, director of the communications program of the Center. It goes without saying that the opinions expressed here are the exclusive responsibility of the authors and in no way implicate our sponsors. This study has benefited from many hours of valuable time given by public servants, researchers, trade unionists, political leaders, and journalists—discretion and prudence oblige us not to mention any names—who generously helped us with research and documentation and allowed us to interview them. To all these people, our heartfelt gratitude.

We would also like to thank our Latin American friends whose interest and assistance enabled us to overcome all of the problems of obtaining information that are inevitable in research of this nature.

Introduction
Unknown Facts Can Hide Others

> This book is a narrative. It is not made for predicting or inventing. It
> relates. The exploration of the world, at the beginning of the 1980s reveals
> so many unknown, essential facts that our only concern here is to deliver
> them. . . .

This quotation is not ours. It consists of the first lines of the introduction
to *World Challenge* by J. J. Servan-Schreiber (1980). We have quoted
them because our approach is the same: *to reveal unknown facts.* . . Unknown facts which hide others!

A relatively unexplored field of research

If one excludes the best sellers by microprocessor crusaders from the
field of serious literature on this theme, there exist very few investiga-
tions on the new communication and information technologies in the
Third World.

    The few studies in existence are mostly concerned with transborder
data flows (see particularly UN Center on Transnational Corporations,
1982; see also Chamoux, 1980; Madec, 1982). More rarely, they analyze
the immediate economic consequences of the automatization of industrial production or the strategies of transnational electronics firms
throughout the world. All these studies are useful, on condition that one
does not wholly accept some of the underlying presuppositions of a good
many of them. For, to read some of these studies on transborder data
flows, one is induced to believe, for example, that if a re-equilibrium of
these flows, presently under American hegemony, could be achieved
through national and international policies, the problem posed to the
Third World by computers and other technologies would vanish, as if by
magic.

1

However, is this not the lot of all functionalist approaches, which neglect the global context and which lead one to think that it is possible to reorganize the elements of a system without touching the system itself?[1]

Studies which take as their point of departure the analysis of work give us a glimpse of other areas left in the dark. No one has yet been able to conclusively show the influence of microelectronics on the supply of jobs. In March 1982, a French economist went so far as to write: "do the little silicon chips that make up the integrated circuits exercise such a power of fascination that the most refined economists lose their heads? We have every reason to think so for it seems to be impossible to find a general consensus as to the effects of micro-electronics on employment" (Pastré, 1982; see Pastré et al, 1981; Fast, 1982). In the absence of absolute certitudes, the domain of economists concerned with the future of work tends to be divided trivially between the clan of "optimists" and the clan of "pessimists."

Evading such decisive problems exposes us all to great risks. These problems predated computers and will survive their rapid expansion. What does the impact of computerization mean, for example, in countries where over 40% of the active population is already outside the circuit of regular work? By dint of isolating technological innovation and considering it as an *exogenous* factor of economic growth after the fashion of what Joan Robinson called, "manna from heaven, given by God and engineers," its place in the evolution of a long term, global economic framework has been forgotten. In short, it has been forgotten that, "the significance of technological progress varies, evidently, from country to country, depending on the type of social organization or the conjuncture considered" (Pastré, 1982, p. 32).[2]

The uncertainties continue when one attempts to evaluate the impact of automation on the implantation strategies of transnational firms in the Third World (see notably Rada, 1981, pp. 41–67; Ernst, 1983). Will cheap labor be replaced by robots working 24 hours a day, demanding neither social security, nor wage increases?

---

[1] A number of studies on transborder data flows and the political propositions drawn from them risk, for these reasons, ending up in the same impasse as the demands for a re-balancing of international press flows and the establishment of a "new international information order."

For a critical analysis of the discussions and strategies of the non-aligned countries in the domain of information, see Mattelart (1983).

[2] As one would expect, the theoretical question is more important than it appears here. The orientations of studies on the impact of computerization on the work process have a direct relation to the way in which the workers' movement conceives of implementation strategies in order to counter effects identified as being negative.

The reduction in the number of components, which in the average television set has decreased from 1200 to 400, has enabled the development of automatic assembly equipment, thus reducing the importance of labor. In 1980, three-quarters of components produced by Japanese firms were automatically inserted on printed circuit boards. By the end of the 1970s, Japanese firms were the only ones to have transferred automated techniques into Third World countries. The transnationals based in other industrialized countries seem to prefer to continue to exploit the advantages of a semi-specialized cheap labor force (see Hoffman and Rush, 1980).

The situation is, however, evolving rapidly, at least in Southeast Asian countries, if we are to believe the results of a study carried out in March 1982 by *Business Week*. Firms like Motorola and Fairchild Camera and Instrument Corporation were in the process of repatriating some production lines to the United States where, "modern computer-controlled assembly of chips costs the same as using Asian labor." In the same study, the international general manager for Motorola's semiconductor group affirmed that, "the trend for the future is for more and more of the assembly to take place in the U.S. or in Europe" (*Business Week*, 1982).

In what could well be a movement of relocating employment on a world scale, all Third World countries are not, however, in the same boat. Obviously South Korea is not the Philippines and Brazil is neither Bolivia nor Paraguay.[3] The emergence of "newly industrialized countries" in the 1970s has definitively weakened the idea of an economically uniform Third World.

---

[3] It is in this context that we must understand the efforts of countries like Hong Kong, Singapore, South Korea, and Taiwan to equip themselves with microcomputer, software, and advanced electronics industries (see chapter 1). At the beginning of 1981, the South Korean government announced a vast research and development plan for semiconductors, aimed at linking the efforts of the state and private industry. Similarly, the Taipei government finances nearly 1000 scientists belonging to the Taiwan's Electronics Research & Service Organization.

Brazil, in the framework of its microcomputer policy, has begun to concern itself with the implications of the automation of the production process. In the report of the Brazilian delegation to the 5th Conference of Latin American Computer Authorities (CALAI), held in Santiago de Chile in November 1981, one could read: "The Computer Aided Design (CAD) and Computer Aided Manufacturing (CAM) systems have become priority targets for the Brazilian government. These systems are vital elements, in at least two strategic sectors: microelectronics and industrial robots. . . Brazil is in the process of developing, in an exploratory project, CAD systems for microelectronics. CAD/CAM systems linked to industry are being studied, and soon a policy which will govern their industrialization and usage in Brazil will be defined." See SEI (1982, p. 45).

On the relation between automation and new forms of dependence, see Bennaceur and Gèze (1980).

The global challenge of the computerization of the Third World

Our research does not attempt to settle the uncertainties that mark preceding studies. It can only record them, for our point of departure and our concerns on the computerization of the Third World are quite simply different. We analyze the evolution of communication and information systems as a global system for the organization of power, but also as a system where various social, cultural and industrial projects confront one another.

The new systems of communication and information, situated at the confluence of computers, telecommunications and audiovisual media are here envisaged as complex and interconnected systems. The neologism "telematics" (from the French word, *télématique*), coined from the contraction of the French *télécommunications* and *informatique,* illustrates this process of synthesis. The convergence of numerous networks, through which flows of information circulate toward a single point, the screen or computer terminal (sometimes confused with the more banal television screen) shows that it is impossible today to isolate the previously separate domains of information-news, information-leisure, information-know how, and information-social control. Information of the type conveyed by the means of mass communication, or information understood in the sense of journalistic raw material is becoming too narrow and restricted a concept to cover the social phenomenon of information.

This very transversality can also be seen in its insertion into the new industrial configurations of advanced capitalism. The big groups of the "information industry" seek to integrate as many links as possible in the chain of electronic information: the industry of strategic information and decision-making, the industry of scientific and technical knowledge, the industry of professional training, the entertainment industry. The technological evolution of electronics itself is marked by a growing interpenetration between the various components of the sector (from the telephone to the computer, including components, products for the general public, and the arms industry).

Information and its technology tend to interfere with every aspect of individual and collective life to the extent that, as a Brazilian engineer metaphorically pointed out, "the difficulty in defining information is similar to that of defining life" (Parente, 1979).

The production, storage, and distribution of information is becoming a fundamental element, and is the objective of the new organizational pattern of the political, economic, cultural, and military apparatuses in almost all societies. This is so much the case that the handling and control of information are increasingly seen—rightly or wrongly—as the basic dynamic elements for overcoming the present crisis, a crisis which is rocking all aspects of society and is forcing the reorganization of groups and classes within each nation, as well as affecting relations between all of the countries of the international community.

This exploratory study tries to answer these questions, taking into account the multidimensional character of information as a raw material, called on to structure the new schema of the planetary order. It is the result of a long study voyage throughout the Latin American continent.

In the course of this investigation seven countries were visited, chosen in terms of their level of technological development and their political, economic, and social interest: Mexico, Panama, Venezuela, Colombia, Peru, Chile, and Brazil. We consulted numerous information centers and public and private archives. We talked with officials of government agencies (Ministries of Communications and Telecommunications, agencies with official commitments to developing a computer policy), directors of firms specializing in this area, and directors of research institutions. We met with directors of electronics and computer firms, professional associations, researchers, university lecturers, and directors of social organizations. We consulted the bibliographies of official bodies and specialists from the information sector. We sought out alternative experiments to those of the authorities. Finally, we evaluated the state of research and the information available.

The diversity of these sources of information—illustrative of the multiplicity of the areas to be covered—gives us a glimpse of the new theoretical challenges in the study of communication as an integral part of the social sciences as a whole.

Four chapters are based on these studies.

The *first* chapter deals with the evolution of the electronics industry for the public at large in Latin American countries, and the place that this infrastructure for the production of transistors, cassette recorders, television sets, etc. occupies in the organization of the transnational economy. It then examines the manner in which these mass products are distributed, particular the videocassette recorder.

The *second* chapter draws up a balance sheet of the state of the three main components of the new systems of communication and information: audiovisual media, computers, and telecommunications, and puts their interconnections into perspective.

The *third* chapter, the key part of this book, develops a typology of the specific forms taken by the computerization process in various Latin American countries. This leads to a reflection on the role assumed by the state, private firms, both local and foreign, the different components of civil society, and, last but not least, the armed forces, in the gestation of a national model of introducing the new communications technologies. This chapter also gives us an opportunity to retrace the contradictory genealogy of communications systems in this part of the world. The first section, which poses certain questions in respect to the evolution of computerization models in Europe, has no other objective than as a point of comparison. It obviously does not pretend to establish a direct line of continuity between Europe and South America.

The fourth chapter considers the structure of the transnational information industry and the methods it adopts in Latin American countries.

Latin America and the Third World

The situation of Latin American countries does not necessarily conform to the image of all of the Third World, even if they share with other African and Asian countries a good many problems in their opposition to the big industrialized countries. Also, the situation of all of the countries making up Latin America is not necessarily the same, although all bear the traces of a long history of confrontation with their powerful Northern neighbor.

The expansion of the new communications technologies reveals both the existence of common questions in the different countries of the Third World and the increasingly large gaps between them.

In March 1982, representatives from African countries gathered in Rome asked: "Will the circulation of data consolidate and reinforce the traditional economic flows on the African continent or does it constitute a controllable means of favoring development projects autonomously centered on a region and on the continent itself?" (IBI/OUA, 1982, p. 3).[4] This question could be posed in unison by all Third World countries. However, differences in economic development within these countries, as well as divergences on a political level, often prevent them from finding common responses and constructing new solidarities. And yet, these new solidarities are essential if the mechanical repetition of the orientation of the present flow of communications, linked as it is to the movements of people and goods (commodities, services, techniques, cap-

---

[4] Other facts revealed in this document: Morocco, well-off in computer equipment compared to the rest of Africa has a total stock of such equipment equal to 0.9% of that of France. In Egypt, in the year 2000, the density of telephone networks will be—if objectives are attained—equal to that of the French network in 1970 (IBI/OUA, 1982).

ital), is to be avoided. This orientation favors relations in the North-South direction, to the detriment of South-South exchanges.[5]

The state of telephonic infrastructure, which ought to serve as the foundation for the development of the new communication systems, demonstrates this heterogeneity in the Third World, regarding which many diagnoses and discourses on the promises of the new technologies thumb their noses. Thus, in 1981 the density of telephones in Africa was 0.4 main lines for 100 inhabitants, whereas this figure is approximately 5.0 in Latin America. Compared to countries south of the Sahara, North Africa is much better equipped: Egypt and Morocco have double the African average of telephones per inhabitant, while the figure in Libya is ten times the African average. Another example: whereas Latin America is moving at an accelerated rate into the international telematic banking system, African financial institutions remain outside this network.

What, then, is a study on the methods of expansion of the new communication and information systems in Latin America likely to contribute to other Third World countries?

First, taken as a whole and in relation to the other sectors of the Third World, Latin America is the region where communication and information systems have so far attained the highest level of development. The process of concentration of the cultural industries and the emergence, in some of these countries, of big, local multimedia groups, show the extent to which the new technologies are becoming increasingly an instrument for the concentration of economic power. This has forced us to break with a unilateral vision of the impact of the new technologies in this corner of the planet, a vision overly inclined to see the Third World as being devoid of all autonomy. It has also forced us to outline our differences with an openly paternalistic ideology, all the more tenacious in that it has made itself polymorphous. This ideology proposes microprocessors as a miraculous exit from underdevelopment and completely erases the sociohistorical conditions in which their introduction takes place in each country. The process of computerization in Latin American countries reminds us that the social forms adopted by these communications technologies and the social uses promoted for them are not independent of the relations of force at work in each nation and on the international scene.

---

[5] An analysis, for example, of international telephone flows in Africa during the 1970s tends, in effect, to prove that half of the international traffic of each country is concentrated in two countries, one in Africa, the other outside, in most cases a European country.

Second, there exists in Latin America a long tradition of critical research on this theme. This research has evolved along with the political and cultural processes at work in this continent. Furthermore, the authors of this book have been intimately linked with this research since the beginning of the 1960s (see for example Martin Barbero, 1982).

The more advanced level of technological development in combination with the state of critical research undoubtedly makes the various Latin American countries useful observatories from which it is possible to open on a new basis a discussion on the relation between development and information technology. This discussion is all the more urgent in that Third World regimes will be increasingly induced to confront, in the specific terms of their own countries, situations similar to those faced today by many Latin American countries.

The Third World and the industrialized countries

What can this study contribute to the careful consideration which is being given to these ideas in the North, particularly in countries like socialist France which, through numerous contradictions, is trying to re-define its relation with the Third World?

In the course of our research, we realized the extent to which French firms specializing in the information industry were present in the vast Latin American market. Theirs was the responsibility for the modernization of certain telephone networks; they were in the forefront of those invited to sponser the launching of national satellites; finally, they were lavishing advice and material on the first videotex experiments. We were also able to see the extent to which telematics is the driving force behind export of the telecommunications sectors. Unlike their more pragmatic Japanese, German, Dutch, Swedish and, above all, American competitors, French firms, accompanied by official statements and documents, offered models of society, or rather models for the restructuring of society, which reflected the mythology cultivated by the Giscardian regime on the redeeming and democratic value *per se* of the technological tools on the market.

Carried out in the months immediately following the victory of François Mitterrand in May 1981, this field trip enabled us to assess the immense hope that the socialist victory aroused in Latin America. Many of the people we spoke to saw this victory as a unique occasion for the beginning of a joint questioning of the unequal relations which mark the technological exchange between the North and the South in this and other areas. This research reminds us, among other things, that the Third World has already developed a viewpoint, both on the sociocultural impact of the new technologies of communication and on their industrial repercussions. We are not referring here, however, to the Third World *en bloc*, but to certain countries and, within these countries, certain groups or individuals belonging either to the circle of scientific researchers or trade unionists. This simple, obvious fact makes it urgent to conceive of a policy of alliances which is capable of distinguishing between a computer demand coming from rich countries, highly credible because highly solvent, and one emanating from groups and peoples attempting to counter the authoritarian logic that follows from the transnational model of diffusion for the new information technologies, or even directly from the transnational model of growth itself. This has forced us, finally, to wring the neck of an ethnocentric image of a miserabilist Third World, hawked by widely different circles, as is illustrated by this commentary in June 1982 by a French journalist, following a conversation with J. J. Servan-Schreiber: "All attempts to help (the Third World) over the last thirty years have more than shown (its ineffectiveness). . . One constructs ultra-modern factories for them but they are incapable of running them because they are not used to them" (*Le Nouvel Observateur,* 1982). *Q.E.D.:* by simplifying the tasks, the microcomputer ought to save them!

In the battle for markets, the discourses accompanying the large electronic, computer, and aerospace firms will increasingly take on a strategic role as the screen or back projection of a whole social and economic project. Will the accompanying discourse and consequently the practice of a nationalized French firm be the same as those of an American multinational, or will they differ substantially in their approach? How can one link a theoretical reflection on the socioeconomic impact of these technologies to a new industrial policy which does not regard Third World countries simply as more or less solvent dumping grounds for factories or products, but rather attempts to associate them with the establishment of a new world economic order that does not merely extend the frontiers of the markets of the North? These questions appear to be essential for all those seeking to link a policy of industrial exportation and cooperation with the South with a cultural policy that takes account of the decisive importance of information and communication systems in the broad sense in the years to come.

Replying to the latter question, posed as it is in terms of a relation with something yet unknown, implies going more deeply into the question and resolving it in the North. For it is only to the extent that one includes users in a democratic debate over telematic choices in the North that one can break with the determinism of technological supply and allow the emergence of a real social demand. Such demand would help to quash technocratic conceptions which, under the banner of the "computerization of society," see the new technologies as a means of preserving the dominance of the industrialized-core countries in international exchange.

Between desires and reality

Affirming that the re-definition of the relations between the big industrialized countries and the Third World is moving massively in a philanthropic direction would be to err on the side of idealism.

The good intentions are admittedly there, as is illustrated by the diagnosis and propositions contained in the speech of François Mitterrand at the Versailles summit of industrialized nations in June 1982. On the strategic place occupied by the new communication technologies in the construction of a new world order, the diagnosis is extremely clear:

> The stake exists, an immense one, for, in the absence of a powerful movement of exchange, the risk of uniformization hovers over every culture and every language.
>
> Communication is being concentrated in every country. A few firms are appropriating the whole of the networks necessary for electronic diffusion. By controlling them, they influence, in turn, the traditional media: cinema, press, and television. The essential part of the new activities in which most of these firms are engaged (production, storage, and processing of information) supposes very heavy investments which lead to a strong concentration.
>
> Already, the two biggest image-banks supply the quasitotality of the world's television stations and over threequarters of all press dispatches come from five agencies. Generalized, this natural tendency will lead, by the end of the decade, to the control of the world communications industry by 20 firms. By cooperating, we shall avoid information being accumulated and processed by a small number of firms and nations disposing of the most rapidly perfected processing and storage systems.
>
> More generally, the diffusion of information developed and controlled by a few dominant countries could lead to a loss of memory and sovereignty on the part of the others, thus calling into question the freedom to think and decide. (Mitterrand, 1982, p.9)

The main principles around which a "world charter of communication" should be organized are also clearly set out:

- affirm the respect for the diversity of languages;
- promote the harmonization of legislation on the subject of information, intellectual property, contractual law, and the protection of individual liberties;
- encourage the setting of common rules for international data exchanges;

- protect the sovereignty of states and their cultural integrity threatened by the new technologies;
- guarantee the countries of the South the means of controlling their means of communication and the messages they convey. (Mitterrand, 1982, p. 13)

In the opposite direction, can be found policies for overcoming the crisis through the technology of the big Western countries, limiting to the meanest share the negotiating terrain for establishing new bases for industrial and technical cooperation between North and South.

In spite of the profound divergences between the United States and a Europe which is less and less inclined to accept its slide into economic and commercial tutelage, the tendency is more towards the consolidation of industrial alliances within the realm of the big powers. France is not excluded as is illustrated by the dilemmas it faces in the reorganization of its electronics industry. Through the size of its market (ten times that of France and half that of the world) and its technological wealth, the United States is becoming a priority site for the internationalization of French electronic firms.

The logic of these reindustrialization policies, namely, the need to conquer external markets, comes into conflict with the need to arrive at a concerted development of the world economy with which the countries of the South are fully associated.

What is more, in the governmental and commercial spheres of the large industrialized countries, there are more and more declarations in favor of a new conception of the international division of labor, based on the dividing line drawn by knowledge. Some go so far as to bring the retention of information and the control of "grey matter" industries into a question of national security. For their part, the new systems of production and diffusion of knowledge have themselves contributed towards the creation of new forms and tactics for guaranteeing the undivided ownership of the information that feeds knowledge. One speaks of the "vulnerability" of the West.

As long ago as 1978, the former French NATO representative unveiled, in the NATO Review, a discourse that other leaders of the industrialized countries often hide under the cloak of dialogue and North-South interdependence:

For the external observer, in the world of today, the West appears as a single entity, characterized, admittedly, by the liberty of its institutions, but more so, undoubtedly, by the highest standards of living in the world. However, this standard of living has been built on an international division of labor inherited from the 19th century and the colonial era. A question of capital importance thus arises: having lost control of energy sources and the principal raw materials, are we now vulnerable and threatened? . . . How will the West, with its high salaries, advanced social legislation and its more restricted outlets, be able to remain competitive? It requires a certain quality and a great deal of faith in the blessings of free trade not to resort to protectionism in one form or another. But sooner or later, the last straw will break the camel's back. . . . A less damaging countermeasure for the West would undoubtedly be to devote itself, more and more, to those activities requiring the most grey-matter and the most advanced level of technology. This is perhaps the beginning of the revolution foreseen by Danzin (Institut de recherche d'informatique et d'automatique, France) and Branscomb (IBM, New York) who argue that the essential raw material of the future will no longer be energy but knowledge. Fortunately, we have excellent trump cards, For, even if it were possible to operate a factory that was delivered in immediate working order, the passage from laboratory to factory requires long delays insofar as human development is concerned, whether it be that of scientists, administrators, technicians, or workers. It is thus possible to assert, from basic, freely available data, that only a few countries are capable of adapting this data to technology and industrial exploitation. In other words, if it were possible for developing countries to acquire our technology, it is almost exclusively in the West that this technology is developed and perfected. Should we envisage a non-transfer of our benefits, if the necessary resources are refused us? (de Rose, 1978)

Diametrically opposed, in appearance, to the argument of the French diplomat, who re-models the world order on the basis of a social and technical division of labor, and thus rigidifies the old disequilibrium, other voices, of an unbridled optimism, see in the transfer of knowledge the outline of a radiant future of the whole of humanity. If one is to believe the French journalist and writer, Jean-Jacques Servan-Schreiber, the only chance of salvation for the Third World is to be found in microprocessors, the last hope for escaping from authoritarianism and hunger at the same time.

Shimmering and gleaming in front of the "miserable masses of the Third World," the personal computer will supposedly, "enable them to pass directly from the neolithic age to the post-industrial society" (*Le Nouvel Observateur*, 1982, p. 64).

By jumping across the ages, the good savages can thus afford the luxury of avoiding all the worries and necessities of production, because, for them, it is definitely not a question of producing the little machines, but one of consuming them! Relates Servan-Schreiber:

People reproach me for wasting my time trying to sell computers to the niggers. Even from a totally egotistical point of view and resting on the terrain of economics, these people do not realize that if we succeed, it is employment in France that we defend. And if to the Africans, you add the Indians, the Chinese, the Arabs, and the peasants of Latin America, then I guarantee you that the problem of unemployment will be solved, because there will be more work than the industrial countries can supply. (p. 65)

For all these prophets who pay no attention to history or to social conditions and propose a "Marshall Plan for computers," without the slightest concern for the symbolic aspect of this "Marshall Plan" which, if it enabled the postwar reconstruction of Europe, also delivered it, trussed and bound, to the United States, not that of Hemingway or Dalton Trumbo, but that of McCarthy and Rockefeller, we are henceforth on the threshold of the "superstruggle of tommorrow." Argues Alvin Toffler:

For today, the single most important political conflict is no longer between rich and poor, between top-dog and underdog ethnic groups, or even between capitalist and communist. The decisive struggle today is between those who try to prop up and preserve industrial society and those who are ready to advance beyond it. This is the super-struggle for tomorrow. (Toffler, 1980, p. 436)

The ideas of Servan-Schreiber have gained widespread acceptance in certain Latin American circles. His *World Challenge* and Alvin Toffler's *The Third Wave* were best-sellers in Caracas, Mexico City, and Rio de Janeiro bookshops in 1981, and more than one high-ranking public servant made them bedside books.

But what is really happening in Latin America? Is it preparing itself to play the role assigned to this type of region by the former French NATO delegate as quoted above? Are there any indications confirming that Servan-Schreiber's panacea is beginning to dawn? How is Latin America preparing itself to confront the technological transformations of the computer era? Do the different countries cherish the same projects? What relative weight should be given to historical and cultural factors in each country in their response to this new challenge launched by the world market? Finally, what importance does this so-called revolution assume in the face of the poverty and oppression that cover a good part of the continent?

Chapter 1

When the Exception Becomes the New Economic Rule

1. The Electronic Industry: A Model in Crisis

De-nationalization, a more and more widespread practice

The exception confirms the rule. In 1979, the Brazilian firm, Gradiente, bought for a song all rights and property of the British high-fidelity stereo company, Garrard, at the time in liquidation. Up until then, Gradiente produced under Garrard license in its factories in Manaos, Sao Paulo, and Mexico City. Since then, Gradiente, after having taken possession of the Garrard headquarters in Swansea, England, has been profiting from the prestige of the British trademark in the 57 countries where it is distributed. The whole operation cost Gradiente a mere 2,500,000 dollars, after an initial negotiating price of six times this figure. Garrard, a division of the telecommunications manufacturer, Plessey, which had been one of the architects of the Brazilian telecommunications network in the 1920s, had been unable to compete with the Japanese firms which had become owners of the principal British audiovisual enterprises. Along with Akaï, Kenwood, Technics, Sony, Sansui, and Pioneer, "Gradiente-Garrard made in Brazil" would from then on become a reputable name in hi-fi stereo systems, not only in Latin America, but also in Europe and the United States.

However, the consumer electronics industry, in Brazil as Latin America as a whole, has followed a path diametrically opposite to that of Gradiente. Pressed by technological competition and the imperatives of the market, most enterprises have finished up as mixed enterprises and, more frequently still, have fallen into foreign hands. Between 1965 and 1975, the share of Brazilian national enterprises in the domestic electrical appliance market fell from 70% to 20%. During these ten years, over 20 nationally owned enterprises passed into foreign control or closed down. In 1975, seven of the eleven firms controlling the color television market belonged to transnational firms. Two of these, Philco and Philips, represented 45% of the market. 80% of the electronic components used in this industry were imported.

17

Referring to national television industries, a U.S. Commerce Department report pointed out in 1976 that, "Colorado, ABC, and SEMP are Brazilian-owned and have no known licensing agreements with foreign manufacturers of TV receivers. With the trend toward laborsaving and solid state technology and in view of the capital required to be a significant competitor in the market place, these firms might find it beneficial to affiliate with American TV manufacturers" (U.S. Dept. of Commerce, 1976).[1]

This denationalization has continued, as is shown by the alliances of SEMP and Toshiba, and Colorado with Telefunken. It has not always followed the advice of the report cited above; the big billboards that abound in the streets of Sao Paulo present the Japanese label as the universal guarantee of quality: "Philco with its Hitachi technology."

Little transfer of technology

Studies carried out in 1975 in Venezuela show that the electronic sector in 1974 comprised 62 enterprises, of which 46 were devoted to the production of goods directly destined for the consumer. 89% of the capital invested was of foreign origin, and 60% of the raw materials and intermediary products were imported. The intermediary products of national origin involved in the manufacture had little or no direct relation with electronics being wood, cardboard, paint, varnish, etc (Giordani, 1976, pp. 19–20).

A Venezuelan economist points out that this sector is increasingly taking on the character of an assembly industry: "This phenomenon is worrying, given that these industries, electronics in particular, are leading ones whose market in our country is in full expansion. Proof of this is the increase of imports and of the percentage they represent in the total of national imports, as well as the plans for extending electrical and telephone services, the trend towards automation in industry, the development of information processing and the growth in the consumption of electrical appliances" (Tirado, 1980, p. 21).

The problem becomes greater when one studies the contracts for the transfer of electronic technology. In a sample of 29 contracts, 62.5% came from the USA, 16.7% from Holland, 12.5% from Japan, and 4.2% each from Germany and France. The characteristics of these contracts are even more interesting. 43% exclude all exportation of products manufactured with transfered technology. 65% contain clauses limiting ac-

---

[1] On the destruction of local electronic industries, see Mirow (1978, pp. 66–69).

cess to technical information. 62% restrict the use of the technology once the contract has expired (Tirado, 1980, pp. 49–51).

The electronics of neo-liberalism

However, it is undoubtedly Chile which offers the most spectacular illustration of the denationalization of the electronic industry, a logical consequence of the economic policy of the Government which wants only enterprises capable of competing with imported products to survive (Salinas, 1979, pp. 128–131). During the 1970–1973 period, local industry underwent a phase of strong development within the framework of a policy of nationalization, supported by the Popular Unity government. The largest firm producing radio and television sets, linked to the American firm, RCA, was nationalized under the name of IRT (Industria de Radio y de Television). Everything seemed to indicate that Chile would become the privileged supplier for the regional market of the Andean Pact (from which Chile withdrew sensationally in 1975).

The philosophy of free competition adopted by the dictatorship had dramatic consequences very quickly. The new order, by suppressing all protection for local production, lowered the customs duties on electronic products. Taxes fell from 120% in 1975 to 10% in 1978. In addition, during 1977 and 1978 national firms themselves tended to pass from the industrial sector to the purely commercial sector. IRT, which, through its subsidiary ILESCO, had manufactured around 85,000 television sets in 1977, had to close its factory at Arica, in northern Chile, in 1978. That year, its total production was no more than 50,000 sets, and it went into liquidation in 1981. The firm Cantolla turned over its factory at Arica to the army and became the principal distributor of Sony. As for Philips, it laid off a large part of its personnel and proceeded to import most of its intermediary products, thus practically transforming itself into an assembly firm.

For Philips it was the end of an epoch which had begun in the 1940s under a strategy of substituting local production for imports, and had led it in Chile, as in other Latin American countries, to produce for the domestic market. The new, transnational stage of economic development has not, however, affected the Dutch firm in any other way. On the contrary, it has enabled it to undergo a rapid reconversion without changing the general nature of its business. At the same time that it transformed its production in Chile, eliminating its local spare parts factory, it became the owner of a television spare parts factory at Juarez (Mexico, near the U.S. border), which it bought from the American firm, General Telephone and Electronics Corporation which also sold the Philco and Sylvania trademarks (Philips, 1980, p. 6).

2. The Paths of Exception of Transnational Expansion

Breaking protectionisms

The new communications technologies penetrating Latin America are reproducing and accentuating the forms of dependence which have always characterized the electronics industry. But also they are using new methods of penetration made possible by the current schema of transnational production. The new forms of dependence they inaugurate result in a redistribution of the place each Latin American country occupies in the region and in the world. This dependence can be explained only in terms of its relation to the establishment of a new international division of labor.

Since January 1981, Sony has been producing its semi-professional U-Matic videocassette recorder in Brazil, under the name Sony-Videobras, in collaboration with the Brazilian firm Motoradio. Sony is producing, for the first time outside Japan, a range of products which includes cameras, monitors, and perhaps in the near future, will include videocassette recorders of the Betamax type for the general public. The fact that the first stage of production is the launching of a semi-professional model and that the first proposed social use is addressed to an untouched market, shows the implicit intention of their use of this new technology of recording and magnetic reproduction. Implicit, but also explicit, are Sony's advertisements in Brazil, which do not beat around the bush: "Its advent marks the beginning of a new stage in the life of Brazilian firms. From now on, directors can count on a sure, flexible and functional means of dominating their business horizons. Videocassette recorders prove their capacity and efficiency for everything involving training programs, educational projects and administrative management."

The development of information technologies in the internal organization of the firm seems to have had control of the workforce as its essential objective. As early as 1924, IBM-France announced on the facade of its repair workshop: "International Business Machines Company: Automatic Registering Equipment for Personnel Control." Even earlier, in 1901, a commercial announcement in the *Almanach Didot-Bottin* lauded a machine created by a German manufacturer from Iserlöhn: "Devices for controlling workers, patented in Germany and overseas. Latest novelty! A new principle! The most rapid, sure, and simple means of controlling the comings and goings of workers, while remaining invisible to them!" (Examples cited in A. and M. Mattelart, 1979, p. 31.)

Even if expressed in the form of hypotheses, additional evidence can be shown by analyzing the phenomenon of the expansion of the production of the semi-professional videocassette recorder in Brazil, and its proposed uses. Our first hypothesis: Sony has learned from the introduction of the microcomputer in Brazil, which showed that the best distribution tactic was to rely on the business sector first (finance, trade, industry, administration). It is not by chance that 30% of all of the minicomputers produced by the national industry and installed in Brazil function in the financial sector, whereas less than 1% are used in educational activities. The second hypothesis is linked to the following question. What type of logic leads transnational firms to set up industries which, to all appearances, compete with industries already implanted in their mother-country? Answer: the transnational way of operating goes beyond national frontiers, and its rationality, in terms of production and consumption, appears only on a global scale. Thus, Sony's manufactures in Brazil not only has the advantage of assuring it the Brazilian domestic market (where Sony has already established itself in a solid position in the sound reproduction sector) and of avoiding the risk of protectionist legislation, but also of opening up a flow of exports towards markets (Europe and the U.S.) that place import quotas on certain countries (Japan in the case of Sony).

The same objective of circumventing limits fixed by legislation lies behind the creation of certain free trade zones, as is shown by the declarations of intention by Chilean directors when they established the free zone of Iquique: "The setting up of mixed Chilean-foreign firms and the use of the Generalised System of Preference (GSP) as a means of reaching the markets of developed countries (North America, Europe, Japan) with products manufactured by firms of which the country of origin is liable to export quotas, opens up real perspectives" (Junta de administración y vigilancia, 1981, p. 5).

Foreign territories on national soil

The microelectronics revolution is reaching an increasing number of Latin Americans through unusual ways which are usually not thought of. By 1982, the majority of countries of the continent sheltered free trade zones. Space and labor are offered on the international market in enticing advertisements: "Low cost Caribbean Assembly: Trinidad and Tobago. Factory space immediately available. Advantages include: 45¢/hour wages; dexterous, English speaking workers; high literacy rate; daily air cargo to USA: round-trip fare only $230 and generous government incentives to establish your own plant. Skills include core-stringing, coil winding and assembly of microelectronic relays, cable harnesses and computer sockets. Write or call: T. T. Electronic Development Corporation" (in *Electronic News,* September 18, 1972).

The free trade zones, also called investment promotion zones, export-processing zones, or free-production zones, are territories established with special provisions within national boundaries. The local government offers the necessary infrastructure for setting up foreign or national industries. It provides the best possible facilities for importing, producing, and re-exporting commodities. To these free trade zones, one should add what are customarily called "world market-oriented manufacturing industries," like the Mexican subcontracting factories or certain Southeast Asian countries, which have some points in common with the free trade zones. These world market-oriented industries are special cases which follow the same strategy of industrialization oriented towards exportation. In spite of its special status, this type of industry is normally considered comparable to the free trade zones, for purposes of understanding the overall situation.

In the free trade zones, firms can import raw materials and semi-finished products freely. They can manufacture, transform, or assemble products for export without restriction. The advantages offered include what are commonly called the "five freedoms": exemption from corporate income taxes, import duties, import quotas, property taxes, and excise taxes. As a foreign territory enclosed within national boundaries, the free trade zone has its own authorities which exercise governmental responsibilities, seeing to the supply of local labor and assuring peaceful working relations. In addition, many free trade zones offer additional advantages for manufacturers, such as: restriction of workers' political and social rights or their total suspension, no minimum wages, no trade unionism, no strikes, and exemption from social security payments. Haiti guarantees foreign investors in its free trade zone: "Political and economic stability over a long term; social progress; education; a large, freely available, low-cost labor force; strict laws regulating work and forbidding strikes." Such advertisements can be found in U.S. business magazines.

Spearheads of the transnational utopia, the free trade zones have become the dream territories of tomorrow for top management. "Free trade zones are like Hilton hotels," raves an enthusiastic American businessman in Seoul. "When you're inside one, you don't know what country you're in, and the hassles of that country don't touch you. It's the businessman's dream. And the workers are polite and obedient and almost look alike—sometimes you wonder if they're Mexicans, Filipinos, Malays, or Arabs" (Ho Kwon Ping, 1981, p. 12).

This managerial euphoria has its other side, well known to workers in these modern ghettos. The American conglomerate, Gulf and Western, which occupies the major part of the free trade zone of La Romana (a state within a state, outside the law) in the Dominican Republic, had the misfortune to have Christian shareholders. The latter, in the course of an Annual General Meeting, denounced the living conditions of workers in the zone.

> The free trade zone is surrounded by barbed wire and guarded by soldiers. Some of these measures are necessary to apply the law, but they are also destined to prevent trade unionists from entering. . . The free trade zone of Gulf and Western is contributing positively to the Dominican Republic in terms of creating employment. However, the capital necessary for the creation of employment is supplied by the efforts of Dominicans. Many of these would prefer a system in which companies were taxed and workers allowed to organise themselves. The advantages, contributions and the administrative efficiency of Gulf and Western in its job creation programmes must be evaluated in relation to this situation. . . Such as it is, the free trade zone can simply be considered as a transit area between Puerto Rico and Haiti or another country where the hourly wages are less than 55 cents. Using the sophism, Gulf and Western has made some progress, but this does not hide the fact that there also exist unsolved cases of workers murdered for having tried to demand a little dignity, and many other cases of workers who work without protesting but who starve. (Frundt, 1980, pp. 89–90)

The outposts of transnational production

The electronics industry is in the vanguard of the process of the geographical redeployment of the infrastructures of production of the world economy. This process, begun in 1965, by 1975 had affected 23 countries on whose territories industries oriented toward the world economy were installed. In 14 of these countries, these industries were installed in free trade zones (Fröbel et al, 1980, pp. 295–321). Present technological production methods involving microelectronics enable the delocalization of the intensive assembly work. Implantation of this work in free trade zones enables the industry to find the abundant labor it needs.

As an element of the strategy of "export-oriented industrialisation," free trade zones have multiplied in the late 1970s. On the threshold of the 1980s, more than 80 were in operation and 40 more were either in construction or on the drawing board. Free trade zones have taken over the role formerly played by so-called, cheap labor countries. The tendency toward concentration of these zones in the poorest countries is clearly evident. These countries hope to integrate themselves into the "industrialised" economy through the establishment of these transnational enclaves.

The new requirements established by the authorities of the countries in which the first factories were installed as the result of industrialised "delocalization" (like Hong Kong, Singapore, South Korea, Taiwan, and, with special political and economic characteristics, Mexico) have provoked a "second wave" of installations of free trade zones in poorer and poorer countries. Furthermore, important differences have become apparent among different trade zones. These illustrate the different levels of social and economic development of the countries in which they are situated. The denunciation of Gulf and Western by its Christian shareholders movingly describes what one could call "unequal development in poverty." Today, this is one of the keys to understanding the Third World. If numerous well-off Dominicans employ Haitian citizens as household servants, then poor Dominicans constitute, in turn, the domestic help of Puerto Ricans, and a large number of the latter work as servants in the United States.

The newly industrialized countries

Comparison is not proof. Latin America is not Southeast Asia, and the mechanical transposition of the lessons to be drawn from the Asian experience would be an error. However, in order to grasp the logic of transnational expansion and the place occupied within it by the free zones, a detour through Asia is essential.

Changes that would have seemed incongruous in 1974 are now commonplace. Singapore, Taiwan, and South Korea are increasing workers' wages. As early as 1979, a public servant of the Economic Development Board in Singapore remarked in jest that it would be abnormal if they continued to manufacture cheap shirts. Raising wages in a country with muzzled trade unions has very precise goals: to try to smash the yoke imposed on industrial development through the exploitation of a cheap labor force; to try to break out of the vicious circle of dependence attached to assembly industries (even if these countries admit having to continue to submit to them for some time); and to try to attract advanced industries with substantial profit margins, able to absorb easily the new wage policy. The industries of advanced technology will certainly continue to benefit from wage rates much lower than those in Europe (and also favorable energy costs), but, in exchange, will have to intensify their efforts for technical and professional training of their personnel.

Consequently, numerous American manufacturers owning subsidiaries in Southeast Asian countries have begun to transfer their factories in order not to lose any of their past advantages. This explains the recent boom of assembly industries in a country like the Phillipines. The minimum wage in this country is $2 a day, whereas in Taiwan, South Korea, and Singapore it reaches $8 or $9 (*Business Week*, 1979).

However, the paths of re-conversion taken in the "first wave" countries—the "newly industrialized countries" (NIC)—are far from being homogeneous. The industry linked to computers has been chosen by Singapore as a springboard for attaining this new economic stage. The key exhibit for the expansion of the transnational model in the Asian region, Singapore presents itself as the largest center of experimentation for the development of the data processing industry in the region. The American company, IBM, and the large Japanese computer firms have been approached for the establishment of what Singapore hopes to see become the strategic nucleus of software development. A large institute with 16 teachers supplied by IBM will attempt to train between 500 and 1000 computer specialists each year.

South Korea has been considered the most successful showpiece and model of development based on exports—but at what price of repression? It has already sketched out a "strategic turning back." Faced with the stagnation of international trade, it has been trying, since 1980, to pass from an extroverted economy to a self-centered one. "A new conception of the model of import substitutions is being sought with a view to guaranteeing an endogenous or self-centered development, a peripheral version of the French theme of reconquering the domestic marketplace" (Michalet, 1982). South Korea's tools are diversification of its commercial partners in order to escape the hegemony of American and Japanese firms, relaunching of small and medium local firms, search for a technology adapted to the requirements of domestic demand and less linked to the imperatives of the world market, while maintaining a dynamic industrial sector of export production. For South Korea now has its own transnational firms, just like Hong Kong, Taiwan, and Singapore.

The irruption of new transnational actors, above all in the area of microelectronics for mass consumption, is overthrowing the schemas of those who saw transnational expansion only as the accumulation of power by a single country. Scenarios are becoming more and more diversified. CBS/Sony, the biggest record firm in Japan, created a mixed firm with

Avon of Hong Kong in 1980 to develop the local market-the biggest in the Far East after Japan-and to record the most well-known singers and musicians of Hong Kong and the Far East as a whole. In September 1981 Magnetic Technology, a subsidiary of the Asian textile group Lai Jun Garment, launched into the massive production of videotapes in Hong Kong, and is in the process of becoming one of the leading world manufacturers. The 40 million meters of videotape produced each month go to Taiwan where they are manufactured into cassettes.

Countries belonging to the "second wave" of zones will not necessarily see a repetition of the "miracle" of the "gang of four," as the privileged groups of Asian countries were called by a Hong Kong journalist. It is understandable that the temptation to believe in this "miracle" is great. This explains the eagerness with which numerous poor countries are opening their territories for the installation of free trade zones.

3. The Free Trade Zones of Latin America

The canal heritage

Following directly in the footsteps of a tradition of commercial trade which began with the colonial epoch, Panama created the free port of Colon in 1948. Numerous factors made Panama a privileged site for the establishment of 2 centers for international commerce, storage, reshipping, and transformation of all kinds of industrial products. In addition to the normal advantages to be found in this type of territory, such as tax concessions or facilities like transport and communication infrastructure, a unique and highly symbolic fact is added: the American dollar circulates freely. Even better, the dollar is, in reality, the currency of Panama. The Panamanian monetary unit is only called the Balboa through pure convention. Its value varies from the American dollar by fractions of cents.

Currently, 365 firms, representing 600 other firms from throughout the world, operate in the free port of Colon. They employ approximately 9,500 people (including 3,200 temporary workers). The movement of capital amounted to four billion dollars in 1980, a tenfold increase since 1970. Only the free port of Miami exceeds the Panamanian free zone for retail business. In 1978, four countries alone accounted for 65% of the total imports from the zone. Japan led with 30%, Taiwan and Hong Kong represented 23%, and the United States 12%. The import and re-export share of electronic products has risen constantly over the years, and reached first position among trade products in 1980. The same year, toys (80% of which were electronic) occupied third place among re-exports. It is also significant that Sony and Canon should have chosen Panama as a distribution center for Latin America. In 1978, the Caribbean region absorbed 16% of the total of re-exportations. Of this 16%, more than 75% was destined for Aruba, Curaçao (Dutch West Indies), and San Andrès (Colombia), with the Dominican Republic absorbing the rest. Venezuela (including the island of Margarita) consumed 10%, Ecuador 8%, and Brazil between 3 and 4%. More than 20 countries from America, Europe, and the East shared the remaining 60%.[2]

A world-renowned center of distribution, exceeded only by Hong Kong, the free port of Colon has been trying, since 1980, to become an important center of production as well. It is not by chance that one of the very first projects was negotiated with a firm from the Far East, a South Korean manufacturer of electronic devices. The possibility of extending Colon's activities into production, which would require the occupation of new territory, was foreseen before the signature of the Torrijos-Carter agreements on the repatriation of the Panama canal. Thus, when the agreements came into effect in October 1979, the territory which passed to Panamanian jurisdiction was to be incorporated into the industrial program for enlarging the free zone.

A new "Bracero plan"

The first projects for free zones devoted to production in Latin America were planned for Mexico and Brazil in about 1965. Apparently, they were based on the same principles and were organized at the same time as their homologues in South Korea and Hong Kong. However, the Mexican and Brazilian free zones developed in a very different socioeconomic context. Whereas, in the two Southeast Asian countries, the policy of establishing "factories for world production" constituted the central axis of a global model of development from the beginning, the Mexican and Brazilian free zones remained, on the contrary, veritable enclaves, because in their national territory, there was already a dominant model of development which had arisen from the crisis of the 1930s, marked by incipient national production to replace imports.

Not only was there a difference between the Asian and South American models, but there was also a difference between the two South American countries. Only the Mexican free zones deserved to be classified as a "free zone of production for export." The bulk of the production of the Brazilian free zones was destined for the domestic market. The Brazilian case is therefore *sui generis*.

By launching a project for the industrialization of zones bordering the United States in 1965, the Mexican government intended, above all, to resolve a social problem. The previous year, the *"Bracero"* (manual laborer) program had come to an end. From then on the United States

---

[2] The statistical information on the canal zone is taken from "The Colon Free Zone," *Statistical Compendium*, Panama, 1980, Zona Libre de Colon, *Memoria 1979–80.*

stemmed the flow of Mexican immigrant workers who had flooded in from the central provinces of Mexico, and sent home those they had welcomed when they had needed their cheap labor. In most frontier towns the rate of unemployment reached almost half of the working population. In a climate of social agitation and land seizures in the area bordering Texas and New Mexico, the region was in danger of becoming a permanent center of insecurity for both Mexico and the United States. American firms, more than happy to seize this opportunity, responded *en masse* to the appeal of President Diaz Ordaz.

Ten years later, 70% of the investments made by American capital in these factories (dubbed *"Maquiladoras"* or "subcontracting factories") were devoted to electrical and electronic goods. On the threshold of the 1980s, the Mexican free zones, which in 1973, had spread to all of the "underdeveloped zones" of the country, included nearly 200 factories for the assembling of television sets, transistors, video games, and other products based on semiconductors, supplying jobs for over 30,000 people. This was a record, for overshadowing the free zones in Puerto Rico, which had 140 factories, and those in Hong Kong and Taiwan, which had 45 each (see NACLA, 1975; 1977).

For almost 10 years the Mexican free zones involved only American firms. Since 1978, they have welcomed Japanese, German, English, and Dutch firms. France, on the other hand, is under-represented. These transnational investors need to have only 35% national participation (in wages, raw materials, etc.) to be eligible for the label, "made in Mexico." They can then re-export the products to the United States, taking advantage of the "most-favored nation" clause for developing countries. By 1982, with some 550 factories and 120,000 workers, the Mexican free zones—most of them concentrated in towns neighboring the United States—represented 10% of all subcontracting in the world and 30% of that of developing countries.

Workers' wages—over 85% of the labor force in the assembly industry are women aged between 17 and 23—are admittedly more than they were in the 1960s, but they are still far below those of American workers. Above all, the type of products they assemble has scarcely changed.

Develop the Amazon?

In 1967, within the framework of the overall development project of Amazonia, a free trade zone was created at Manaos, the capital of the region. The objective was to install, in the Brazilian northwest, "a commercial, industrial, and agricultural center, bringing together economic conditions likely to favor an autonomous regional development." In 1981, the gross industrial product of this zone was estimated at 2 billion dollars. In 1980, 188 industrial projects, having created more than 45,000 jobs, had been established, with 56 new firms, amounting to 14,000 supplementary jobs, in the process of being set up.[3]

The free trade zone of Manaos seems at first sight, to have special characteristics. The criteria governing its creation were decidedly different from those which generally govern the installation of these enclaves. On the one hand, it was conceived of from the very start as a device for the incorporation of foreign technology. On the other, it has increasingly used electronic components manufactured in Brazil itself.

The electronics sector is carving out the biggest share of the current industrial production of the zone, with 16% of the installed firms and 34% of the employment. It is interesting to note that 90% of the electronic products from this zone are in the leisure domain. Statistics on color television production allows us to measure the extent of this phenomenon. In 1976, Manaos produced 254,000 color sets, compared to 392,000 for the whole of the rest of Brazil. In 1980, production in Manaos reached 1,050,000 units, while that in the rest of Brazil amounted to only 180,000 units. These figures speak for themselves. In 1980, Manaos produced 2.3 million transistors and 1.9 million pocket calculators (400,000 in 1967). Manaos produced 84% of the national production of radios, 90% of calculators, and more than 81% of sound equipment. Mexico, Argentina, and Venezuela are the principal importers of Brazilian electronic products. The major share of the production, however, is absorbed by the national market.

An analysis of the role of the Manaos free trade zone, carried out by the CNPQ (National Center for the Scientific and Technological Development of Brazil) has shown that the characteristics that make Manaos appear to be a special case are more appearance than reality. Manaos respects the essential rules of the industrialization strategy promoted by UNIDO (United Nations Industrial Development Organisation), which serves as a launching pad for the installation of free trade zones throughout the world. Writes the CNPQ: "The system of fiscal benefits, based on the free importation of goods, and tax exemption for the commercialization of products has led to the installation in Manaos of an industrial structure that has very little to do with the economy of the region." Similarly, measures aimed at encouraging the participation of national capital have been neutralized by the formation of mixed enterprises which, in the last instance, have involved a growing de-nationalization. Concludes the CNPQ: "The free trade zone has not benefited

---

[3] Statistical information on the Manaos free trade zone is taken from *O Globo,* May 20 and 26, 1981; *O Estado de Sao Paulo,* June 26, 1981.

national industry. Up until the creation of the zone, the segment of electronic consumer goods was dominated by national firms. These held on, in spite of the difficulties of importing components and the crampedness of the national market which, apparently, does not arouse much interest from transnational capital . . . A very particular concept of 'national industry' of which the criterion was to be domestic production, independent of the origin of the capital, was thus forged in the country."[4]

Although coming from another point of view, the testimony of the writer, Marcio Souza, a native of the region, is along the same lines: "What makes the most impression in the case of the Manaos free trade zone is the way in which the dictatorship has put an entire city and its people, whose opinions were not asked for, at the service of the interests of international monopoly capital. In this way, it has put a peripheral industrial enclave on the outskirts of the city of Manaos which is highly dependent on the exterior . . . An intimate, meaningful relation exists between the free zone and the dictatorship. One could go so far as to say that all free trade zones, wherever they are to be found, are due to an act of force imposed by a dictatorship" (Souza, 1980, p. 5).

A way out for Pinochet?

In 1975, the Pinochet government decided to create a free trade zone at Iquique in the North of Chile, 1,600 kilometers from Santiago. Known throughout Latin America as a symbol of workers' struggles at the turn of the century, Iquique was incorporated into the new development model imposed by the economic project of the dictatorship. The arguments made to justify the new zone could not be clearer. "Although a development plan concerned with the special characteristics of the area would have advised other paths, strategic requirements of the moment have determined this choice. The geographical characteristics of Tarapaca (the province to which Iquique belongs) are such that any model of development for this region can only be based on the exploitation of its natural resources. (However) the government has decided to create an instrument of development capable of slowing down the tendencies observed in this key region, tendencies which could lead to an irreversible process of socioeconomic deterioration, arising from a particular quality given by the border character of this region" (Junta de administración y vigilancia, 1981, p. 1).

Planned in three phases, the Iquique operation started in 1981. The

---

[4] Extracts published in *Jornal do Brasil*, January 26, 1981, p. 12.

first two phases, the commercial and industrial creation stages, have already been carried out. Only the third, the export phase, remains. Its objective is to make Iquique a supply center of foreign goods for the whole Southern Cone of America. In this respect, the Junta responsible for the administration and surveillance of the free zone hides neither its intentions nor its projects: "Given the results obtained up until now, the ZOFRI (free trade zone of Iquique) can be considered as one of the most rapidly developed free trade zones in the world. However, the real challenge has only begun, for in the future, it will have to fight step by step in order to carry off the markets of the whole of South America against the competition of Colon in Panama, Manaos in Brazil, Baranquilla in Colombia, Internacional in Panama, etc. . . Here we are only mentioning the other successful experiences in Latin America and have not taken into account future installations of free trade zones in Peru and Ecuador" (Junta, p. 2).

Between 1977 and 1980, sales from the Iquique zone increased from 251 million dollars to nearly one billion dollars. Of the 12% of sales to the exterior, two thirds are destined for Bolivia and the rest, in decreasing order, to Peru and Argentina. The 373 commercial firms and the 17 industrial firms of the zone employ a labor force of 3,300.

The free trade zones of Colon, Mexicali, Juarez, Manaos, and Iquique are only the most well-known knots in an ever expanding network whose mesh is developing and consolidating the new transnational power. Latin America has already been marked in many places: Barbados, Colombia, Costa Rica, Dominican Republic, Peru, Ecuador, El Salvador, Guatemala, Haiti, Honduras, Jamaica, Dutch West Indies, Puerto Rico, Saint Lucia, Trinidad and Tobago, Uruguay, Paraguay, and Venezuela. The uses of these free ports and zones are multiple, but all contribute to the reinforcement of the network: commercialization or industrial production; manufacture of finished products; internal, regional, or international consumption; subcontracting of elements from outside; or manufacture of components. All are chain links of a long chain which escapes from these countries' control.

4. Illegal Videocassette Recording

The smuggling networks

What role do the free ports and zones and the other non-traditional mechanisms of commercialization play in the distribution of the new communications technologies and the use made of them by consumers? Why is it that in some Latin American countries the number of electronic devices, like the videocassette recorder, owned by inhabitants reaches percentages equal to those of developed countries?

There were an estimated 300,000 videocassette recorders in Venezuela in 1981. In Brazil, in spite of the strong obstacles against importation, it was estimated that there were 50,000 units in July 1981 and 150,000 in March 1982. The per capita world record belongs to a tiny Caribbean territory, the Cayman Islands, a banking free zone, where 22% of households own video recorders.

However, it is difficult to obtain reliable statistics for Venezuela and Brazil because of the large number introduced, as in the rest of Latin America, through smuggling. This activity, which has long been important in the formation of Latin American economies and cultures, appears to play a key role in the expansion of the electronics market. No-one has been able to prove it, but it is common knowledge that the free ports and zones play an important role in smuggling networks. Of course, we cannot cite names, but anyone in Caracas, Mexico City, or Sao Paulo can acquire video recorders hawked in the street, in hotels, and in offices. The Brazilian magazine *Veja* testified to this in a front-page investigation entitled "The invasion of the videocassette": "There are two ways of acquiring a videocassette recorder; either address oneself to a well-known smuggler or bring it back from a voyage in one's suitcase. A considerable black market has been organised. It is estimated that today the video recorder is the number one sales product of smugglers, having taken over from Scotch."

If one wants to travel without carrying the contraband item in one's luggage, there are ways of receiving it at home. "If a buyer wishes to take advantage of a tourist trip to the USA to acquire a video player, he only has to have confidence in the illegal system of international trade. All he has to do is to buy it at the current price in a shop in Miami, or one of the big department stores on Broadway or on 46th Street in New York (the most frequented by Brazilian buyers) and indicate the address where the item is to be delivered in Brazil. This system works. The seller is in no way compromised and the deliverer, last link in the contraband chain, only touches his share when the item is delivered to the front door. Then he asks for 400 dollars per video recorder."[5]

At the same time, but in much larger numbers, the smuggling of videocassettes is also growing. Here, the law is flouted twice; before crossing frontiers by "exceptional" means, the videocassettes have been pirated, i.e., recorded without authorization. The free zone of Colon in Panama serves literally as a shop window for the distribution of videocassettes. Anyone strolling the streets of the zone can contemplate the immense shelves where films making up the whole history of the cinema are displayed, including the latest productions. On their aseptic packaging, they bear no mention of origin. For $19 a unit (on the condition of buying more than 100), one can in a single shop choose between 670 films in all categories in Spanish, 5 Disney films (also in English), 8 Arab films, 88 triple X films (i.e., porno films) and much more in English, making a total offer of 1500 titles.

No frontiers, no states, no subjects

Other more skilled, yet equally successful, contraband networks record television programs in Miami, both the network channels (advertising included) and cable stations. These are reproduced and sold at low prices in countries like Colombia, where this type of commerce is particularly flourishing.

It is not by accident that the Colombian province with the biggest density of electronic products, also produces the most marijuana and cocaine. These products both take the same routes "of exception." But are these really exceptional in Latin America? In the same way that contraband played a key role in the formation of the economy from the

---

[5] *Veja*, Sao Paulo, July 22, 1981, p. 41. At the beginning of 1982, the Government authorized the selling of the first mass-market videocassette recorders manufactured by the Japanese firm, Sharp (associated with a Brazilian firm) in the free trade zone of Manaos. In March 1982, the price of this videocassette recorder manufactured in Brazil rose to 390,000 cruzeiros, i.e., three times as expensive as in the industrialized countries, whereas a contraband item comes to 200,000 cruzeiros.

beginning of the colonial period, and the way the creole bourgeoisie, developed by breaking with the legality instituted by the Spanish crown, a new normality is being constituted today through "illegal mechanisms" tolerated by the existing systems. It is becoming commonplace to see a Bolivian Indian in the Iquique free zone bring out from under her sixth skirt a wad of dollars to buy electronic products to smuggle back home. In the south of Bolivia, entire villages see their everyday life transformed by the introduction of sophisticated electronic devices which were impossible to obtain not long ago. Leaping over the chasm of centuries, islets of transnational culture are being implanted in the middle of thousand-year old traditions and are gnawing away at them from the inside. Let us add that the money needed to pay for these contraband items often comes, in turn, from another illegal business, the drug traffic.

Like the contraband networks they nourish, the free zones are part of a growing underground economy which heralds the decline of traditional forms of legality. Transnational power is implanting itself on the ruins of a legal system that the old liberal bourgeoisie envisaged as eternal. It is reconstructing a new order on the basis of the old principles from the colonial past: no frontiers, no states, no subjects. Electronics is the royal road for the construction of a new transnational hegemony which is imposing itself by reviving any method history can offer.

Profile of users

In this situation, where distribution channels are so unusual and varied, who, when all is said and done, actually buys videocassette recorders? How are they used (Time Inc., 1981, pp. 4, 5, and 11)? Compared to European and American consumers, Latin American users are older: averaging 38.3 years old, as against 37 in the U.S., and 35.1 in Europe. In relative terms, this difference is greater than it appears, as the demographic pyramids of Latin America are considerably younger than those in Europe or the U.S. As for the mean annual income of video recorder owners, in Latin America it is $52,500, compared to $32,950 in the U.S., and $27,450 in Europe. In Latin America a video recorder purchaser has an income ten times that of the average income of the population. This relation is only 2:1 in Europe and U.S.

It is estimated that 76% of Latin American video recorder owners buy prerecorded videocassettes, whereas only 48% of American consumers and 41% of European consumers do. On the other hand, only 28% of Latin American users record television programs when they are on the air, whereas this percentage reaches 67% in Europe and 85% in the U.S.

These figures, from the marketing study service of *Time,* allow us to draw at least two conclusions. First, at least as far as Latin America is concerned, new technologies like the VCR only accentuate the social disparity between consumers of electronic devices. Second, the way these items are used (generally the re-showing of television programs or pre-recorded films) contradicts the arguments of advertising promotion which presents this new technology as a means of liberating oneself from being dependent on television and increasing one's personal creativity. A more precise evaluation of the phenomenon would require answers to certain additional questions. What programs do Latin American users buy? Does their choice resemble that of television programing? Does the time given over to watching videocassettes replace that of television? If so, how has this change come about? Does one watch a pre-recorded program and a television offering in the same way? Do users change their habits when they have the possibility of recording programs which can be watched later, at a time of their choice?

The electronic sequence

The videocassette recorder constitutes the first rung of a new sequence of electronic devices. A new stage, qualitatively different from that of the past, it creates an everyday environment which is a prelude to the computerized household of the future.

All Latin American countries are not at the same stage in the electronic sequence. Within the same country, different sectors of society are not necessarily affected in the same way. Video recorders, microprocessors, electronic toys, television games, CB radios, detection and surveillance devices, and electronic eye door openers have a different effect on each country.

It is certain that electronic devices are penetrating almost every sector of society, but the chasms that separate these sectors (not reducible to economic inequalities alone) are not narrowed, but on the contrary are widened. The unequal possession and use of these devices marks, even more clearly than before, the differences between the different social sectors. Those sectors which feel threatened now have new objects to reinforce separations and discontinuities.

A person of average means, living in Caracas, told us: "The video recorder is replacing my nights out. The city has become so dangerous; rather than run the risks of the street, I prefer my children to watch films at home rather than go to the cinema." A large number of buildings in Caracas are equiped with doors that are opened by remote control from cars. The obsession with individual security is beginning to regulate everyday life. The outside is seen as a risk, and people who wander there automatically become suspect. The home is increasingly becoming a refuge in which to protect oneself from outside danger. As the growing series of electronic devices expands, the breach between indoors and outdoors is widened. Reclusion in the home underlines, in turn, the separation of social groups. From greater distances, the holders of social and economic power are creating situations of violence which are manifested in many ways and are leading to new forms of isolation and to a dependence on electronic devices for personal security.

Electronic devices are modified and used according to specific conditions of each society and are bringing together, in an apparently arbitrary fashion, geographically distant countries. Caracas has much more in common with Los Angeles than with Lima, and very little with Paris, where, in well-off suburbs, a dog can still be useful as a means of security. To think that the adoption of new communications and information technologies is only the result of the determinism of technological supply is to risk ignoring the numerous social determinations that make the social uses of these technologies admissible and credible.

Chapter 2

How the New Technologies Link Up with the Old

1. A Forgotten Genealogy

The first information revolution

Very few studies take into account the role played by communications systems in the sociocultural development of nations. We know very little, in fact, about the way in which the capitalist mode of communication, defined as a specific mode of production, circulation, and exchange of commodities, messages, and people, was established. And yet one could write a recent history of Latin America on the basis of the development of its railway networks, telegraph and telephone networks, and, more recently, its audiovisual systems.

The Cuban, Moreno Fraginals, one of the rare historians of the subcontinent to have studied the place of information and telegraph networks in the configuration of a local economy (in this case, that of sugar), has shown in minute detail the gestation of the mode of communication of modern capitalism, based on the needs of the flow of capital and commodities. His study merits being quoted at some length:

> The monopoly in the transport of information is symptomatic. From 1840 on, telegraph lines, uniting the principal Cuban sugar-producing zones, were installed by American technicians with American material and capital. Without much ado, the telegraph complex of the island was then linked with the American telegraph complex by underwater cable, inaugurated on 9 September 1867. . . The modern telegraph system, uniting European markets to each other, American markets to each other, and later, through underwater cables, England to the Continent (1851), Cuba to the USA (1867), and the USA to Europe, contributed much to the revolution of commercial practices. It gave a push to the world market. By reducing communications that previously required weeks, to a minute, it forced the acceleration of methods of obtaining, processing, codifying, and decodifying information, thus laying the foundation of what, decades later, was to be called "data processing." It was on the stock exchange that the consequences of this new mode of information transportation was felt. It had to reorganize itself everywhere, its rules having become archaic

overnight. Telegraph and underwater cable provided the necessary conditions of communication for the expanded development of the stock exchange . . . Like the stock exchange, the cable was also a fundamental instrument of neo-colonial domination, but not as a business in itself. Actually, as a firm applying a fixed rate for transmitting messages, the exploitation of the transatlantic cable would have been an irrational investment, without any chance whatsoever of breaking even. Very quickly it resulted in losses and its administration became either state-owned or state-subsidised. The fundamental interest of the cable lay elsewhere: to put the markets of raw materials within arm's reach of finance capital. Intermediary firms disappeared very quickly, and large-scale transnational firms, with whom any competition was impossible, began to appear. The defeatist acceptance of this brutal transformation by businessmen of the old school is impressive even today. In a prestige publication such as *The Financial News* of London, reproduced in *The sugar cane* of Manchester in 1888, one could read this astonishing paragraph: "In the good old days, commodities rarely produced losses, except in times of great panic. Tradesmen, even when they speculated far and wide, had existing commodities in warehouses and ports close at hand. Prudence, prediction, and intelligence were rewarded. The introduction of steamships changed all that, and the telegraph has completed the revolution. Exclusive information, laboriously acquired, which formerly brought an intelligent merchant a profit, has today become public property from the moment it appears. It is available at literally the same time to the audacious speculator as to his competitors; this is now the rule. . ." In parallel with the reduction in the transport time of commodities and the communication of information, it was necessary to accelerate procedures of market intervention. Information itself became more and more abundant and complex, with more variables to manipulate and more parameters to evaluate. It was no longer possible to rely on a single source of information as before, or on news from ship captains. (Up until the end of the first half of the 19th century, ship captains of trading firms fulfilled the role of confidential couriers.) Information, its acquisition and processing, became an activity of specialists, carried out by technicians, using mathematical methods of analysis applied to the prediction of a conjuncture. (Moreno Fraginals, 1978, pp. 24–26)

These observations, which suggest the importance of unequal trading mechanisms on the forming of a communication system in the Caribbean region, do not exhaust all of the questions that can be posed on the origins of the model of social implantation and the institutionalization of communication technologies in this part of the world.

The impasses of an a-historic analysis

The lack of analyses on the genealogy of communications systems in Latin America has frequently overshadowed their real significance in the formation of the state and of civil society (Mattelart, 1979a and 1983). By placing an absolute value, as is normally done, on the variables "private" or "public," "commercial" or "non-commercial," in listing communication systems, one risks making two errors.

The first, in which we can detect the mark of a certain "economism," consists in seeing systems of communications, whether the public or private, simply as mechanisms for the reproduction of an economic model. This view often leads to the homogenizing of systems which function quite differently. Certain theories, which, for example, see the fundamental role of the mass media as "selling an audience" to advertisers, leave aside the complex articulation between the market and the political institutions which construct a consensus among citizen-consumers. Furthermore, these theories neglect the contradictions that are developing inside the different communication systems, according to the importance assumed by the action of the different actors of civil society, at any given moment.

The second error, which reduces the mass media to their ideological function, results from an abstract vision of the state. This conception tends to obliterate the capitalist mode of production and the social contradictions it creates. It also tends to neglect aspects which are less obviously ideological, thus envisaging the functioning of the different social institutions, where the common will or consensus is discussed and constituted, without taking into consideration the zones of conflict, mediation, and negotiation between the various groups and social classes which are established within the state apparatus.

These two congenital malformations of research on the means of communication, which have their roots in a dualist conception of power, refer back to a long political heritage. They illustrate the incapacity of certain sectors of the progressive forces to conceive of the functioning of the means of mass communication outside of the schemata of "manipulation theory." Television, radio, the press, and the cinema are seen as tools directly manipulated by the authorities for the automatic reproduction of their norms, values, models, and signs, without also being seen as places for the production of power. More importantly, this dualist conception comes down to a lack of analysis of civil society and, beyond this, to the very notion of democracy, both in its general and particular senses. Like liberty, democracy is not postulated, but conquered!

An examination of the genealogy of the communication systems would show that each country is unique. In Chile, television was born within the universities and subsequently was developed by a national state network. (Unlike other Latin American countries, the two networks, university and public television, compete on equal terms and capture roughly identical audiences.) In Mexico, television is the result of private enterprise, although the state and the university do control a small minority of the channels. In Venezuela, television began as an experiment carried out under state sponsorship, from which private enterprise profited and developed commercial television. Although both were directed by equally authoritarian regimes, Chile and Argentina (until 1983) did not follow the same policy in audiovisual communication. Chile retained its television under public ownership (radios have always been private), while Argentina was returning its radio and television stations, nationalized under Peronism, to the private sector.

The manichean and a-historical vision which has crept into many analyses of communication systems carried out in Latin America, studies marked by the Althusserian theory of "Ideological State Apparatuses" (widely distributed in Latin America during the struggle against the functionalist current of American sociology) had its counterpart in an abstract vision of the language of the media. Semiological analyses, the initial merit of which was to bring out the materiality of ideology, suffered, in Latin America as elsewhere, from the illusion that everything was reducible to a linguistic corpus, as if this confinement within discourse could take account of the totality of the social mechanisms at work in the phenomenon of communication. In both cases, the notion of *process* was left out in attempts to understand the role played by the communication systems in the concrete formation of social mechanisms.

Different histories

All systems of communication do not necessarily reproduce the hegemony of the dominant sectors. In order to understand the actual role played by communication within each nation, it is necessary to know their history in detail.

The history of the cinema in Latin America, for example, reveals the different perspectives from which the various social sectors and states have approached it. It many Latin American countries, the dominant classes have little interest in developing a local cinema. This explains in part why the cinema was able to grow on the fringes and remain in the hands of the progressive sectors for long periods of time. This was notably the case in Chile, Peru, and Colombia, among others. In Mexico, where the appearance of the cinema industry coincided more or less with the cinema's invention, the industry developed concurrently with the growth of nationalist sentiment and was the mode of expression chosen by the hegemonic sectors to translate their anxieties and their vision of the country. In Venezuela, on the other hand, the cinema industry had to wait for the vacuum left by the failure of the guerrilla movement at the end of the 1960s before the state begun its development. It was, in fact, the themes of this failure that were dealt with. The intellectual sectors of the petite bourgeoisie, in which political resistance had developed in privileged fashion, were invited into this new field of cultural creation. (Let us add in passing that it is also from this sector that the administrators of a new political project that bears the marks of technocracy, are recruited.)

All communication systems do not have the same importance in each country and the contradictions involved in their operation are not the same in each country. The very conception of the liberty of the press varies from one institution to another, and from one regime to another. All liberal democratic states do not conceive of press freedom in the same way; nor do all dictatorships.

Numerous examples, drawn from the past and recent history of various Latin American countries, show that liberty of expression may be treated differently by different media. Undoubtedly, one of the most eloquent examples is that of Brazil at the end of the 1970s, with the timid beginning of the "democratic opening." If the freedom of the press in newspapers and journals appeared genuine, this was not the case with radio and television. These modern devices, the only ones to reach the vast majority of Brazilians, were the real means of constructing consensus and cultural hegemony, and thus they continued to be subjected to very close censorship. According to a study carried out at the time by university lecturers at Sao Paulo, 40–60 million Brazilians received the news through radio and television. Barely 1 million read of it in the press, and of this number, only 200,000 consulted the political columns. The vast majority of these readers were informed through other sources before reading their newspapers. Moreover, the Brazilian press is regional, whereas television has a national network.

One could remark, however, that in all communication systems, one of the institutionalized models of technology plays a uniting role in relation to the others, and gives the whole a relative coherence. The essentially integrative nature of computer technology, which increasingly appears as a new pacesetter for all the elements of the system, will result, without a doubt, in a new hierarchy. That is, there will be a reorganization of all of the segments of this system of communication and a redefinition of the function of each segment in the production of consensus.

One of the factors which differentiates the model of social implantation of communications technologies of the past (like radio and television) and that of the data processing technologies, is the fact that the former did not arrive in Latin America until after they had become established models in their countries of origin. This was true to such an extent that Latin American countries often served as a dumping ground for out-of-date equipment, providing a windfall for foreign suppliers. In the transnational era, things have changed. The new systems of data processing were implanted in Latin America at almost the same time as in the producing countries. The logic of the capitalist system demands a planetary expansion for its well-being. Latin America now often serves as a guinea pig for the development of the new systems introduced by the transnationals. Argentina, along with Brazil, is one of the first countries in the world in which the application of optical fibers has been deployed. Countries are no longer defined in terms of the place they occupy on maps, but in terms of the interrelations maintained by the different elements of the transnational complex.

In the conclusion to a report on the situation of the computer market in Venezuela, carried out by a consulting agency in 1979 at the request of the US Department of Commerce, one reads: "the technology time lag between the U.S. and Venezuela has shortened considerably. New systems are often introduced here within one year of their commercial baptism at home. Venezuelan customers have become sophisticated; they know about, expect, and are willing to pay for the most recent usable technical advance, and their attitude has made the industry very competitive" (Final Report, 1980).

2. Audiovisual: The Contagious Multimedia Model

The transversality of the sector

The integration of the different material forms assumed by the flow of information reflects the structure of the new monopolist concentrations. Image and reflected object work dialectically to resuscitate the old question; where is the original reality to be found? The overlappings of computer networks are the symbol of the cross-stitchings woven between firms producing cultural commodities and information. In the advanced capitalist countries, multiple alliances between hardware and software manufacturers, or between the different segments of the cultural industries, have led to the formation of diversified cultural conglomerates. A horizontal and vertical model of integration tends to govern the operation of the entire information industry. The arrival of new systems of communication (satellite, cable television, telematic networks) puts the old notions of public service and public monopoly in jeopardy and results everywhere in a redistribution of partners.[1]

In the meantime, what is happening in Latin America in the industrial production of culture and information? What steps have been taken by the private groups controlling the field of communication to incorporate the new technologies? It is obvious that the inability to create and produce hardware does not account for the existence of conglomerates in Latin America that are found in the industrialized core-countries. The model reoccurs, however, but with its own characteristics. We are currently witnessing a growing "privatization" of the institutions of cultural production, or at least discussions on the timeliness of this privatization.

---

[1] On the integration of the information industry, see Mattelart (1979); A. and M. Mattelart (1979); Flichy (1980); Schiller (1981).

In countries where the private sector has already established its supremacy, we are seeing the expansion of local conglomerates which are absorbing the different activities linked to culture and information. In the more concentrated groups, the new technologies are offering the opportunity to develop still further the current tendency toward the monopolization of information.

The strong influence, from the beginning, of the American commercial model of radio-television and the excessive growth of an advertising apparatus largely controlled by the big transnational firms are undoubtedly the principal features which define, to varying degrees, the majority of the audiovisual systems in the countries of Latin America. But we cannot end our analysis there, nor limit ourselves to the vague evocation of what constitutes only the framework of a general overdetermination. In each country, the radio-television institution has acquired its own particular physiognomy which reflects differences in the social relations of force, at the national and international level, and in the way in which mass communication networks are articulated with the whole of civil society and with other agents of the socialization of the citizen and consumer. Finally, it reflects the degree to which the state and the interests of the private sector conform.

An aggressive televisual capitalism

The degree of concentration of the media in the hands of private groups brings together countries as disparate as Brazil and Mexico. The fraternal relations that exist between Rede Globo (based in Rio de Janeiro) and Televisa (in Mexico City) create not only corporate links, but also a common model of expansion and cultural policy which requires the most modern technology.

Rede Globo, the largest channel of Brazilian television, created in 1965, belongs to the Globo Organization, which includes the newspaper, *O Globo,* one of the leading in the country, founded in 1925; the Globo radio system, inaugurated in 1944 and composed of 17 stations on the AM and FM bands; a publishing firm, Rio Grafica Editora Ltd; the Globo system of audiovisual recordings (SIGLA); the electronic industry Telcom; a show-business promotion firm, VASGLO; the Global art gallery, and last, but not least, the Globo television network which comprises 5 broadcasting stations, 36 affiliated stations and hundreds of retransmission stations. Fifty-five hundred technicians and professionals work for this chain, which employs a total of 25,000 people.

Rede Globo covers all Brazilian territory, and its audience is estimated at 75% of the national audience, whatever the broadcasting time. Its programs, especially its serials, are exported to more than 50 countries. Its production is such that imports account for no more than 2 mass-audience programs out of 10. In 1978, Rede Globo created the Roberto Marinho Cultural Foundation to be, according to its own definition: "alongside Brazilian communities in the search for solutions to problems linked to the common good" (TV Globo, 1980, pp. 3–8).

Rede Globo does, however, have rivals even if they are rarely in a position to destabilize its monopoly. In 1981, the magazine *Manchete* (owned by the Bloch group) bought up Rede Tupi, the second biggest television network, which had closed down shortly beforehand because of financial difficulties. Successful in its bid (the large publishing company, Abril, had also made an offer), the Bloch publishing group, which owns large interests in other sectors of the cultural commodities industry, found itself the owner of television channels in at least four of the biggest states of Brazil.

Media concentration in the image of the one-party state

In Mexico, Televisa, a group established in 1973, owns four television channels with 61 retransmission stations which cover almost the entire country. Out of a total of 55 million viewers, this network attracted 41 million in 1979, or 7 million households. The network has 2,400 employees and 2,300 temporary workers, without counting the monthly contracts which link it to about 500 actors, 30 producers, 60 assistants, and several hundred others.

The 47 firms that make up Televisa Ltd. run the gamut of the culture industries. Its exported television programs represent 24,000 projection hours a year and are sent to the United States, Central America, South America, the Caribbean, and, recently, the Arab countries. In 1979, a stock of more than 70,000 hours of programs and documentaries made since 1962, made Televisa the owners of "the biggest videotheque of the continent." Moreover, its studios produce 2,000 television advertisements a year, some of which are for export. Its network, Univision, uses microwaves to transmit signals as far as Houston, Texas, so that they can then be relayed by an American satellite. In this way Televisa broadcasts 21 program hours a week from Mexico City to the 11 U.S. cities with the biggest Hispanic populations. More than 18 million people are thus able to be in contact with Mexico in their mother tongue each day. The television network is completed by two cable television firms. The first, Cablevision Ltd, transmits English language programs directly from the United States for Mexico City viewers. The second, Galavision, broadcasts eight hours of programs daily in Spanish to viewers in Puerto Rico and in the U.S.

Televisa also owns five radio stations, including the largest one in the country; five publishing houses of books and magazines (womens' and TV), whose print-runs are the highest on the Mexican market; nine show business firms, which extend from the theatre to the football club "America" and include pop singers and cinema networks; three cinema production firms including one exclusively given over to cartoons; four record companies; a tourist company, etc., etc. Like Rede Globo, Televisa also owns a cultural foundation which bears its name. The foundation's mission has been clearly defined in the following terms: "Televisa, always concerned with the distribution of culture, has created the cultural foundation Televisa, a civil non-profit association, which brings together 12 of the most brilliant Mexican intellectuals and is devoted to the following tasks: 1) to plan the methods to be used by television for secondary teaching with programs like *Introduction to University;* 2) to recover archaeological pieces from overseas and restore them to the national heritage; 3) to encourage talented young people with scholarships; 4) to organize an Archive of the Image with more than 50,000 half-hours of videocassettes, owned by Televisa."[2]

Televisa is also a patron of the arts through the Rufino Tamayo museum, recently created in the Mexican capital; finally, thanks to the Archive of the Image, it has an Institute of research and historical documentation.

The polymorphous ramifications of Televisa probably make Mexico a unique case in the history of radio and television. This degree of monopolization of television, in the hands of a single private group, can probably not be found in any capitalist country. Everything has happened as if the single party political structure which characterises the Mexican regime has been transposed to the commercial television system, avoiding, of course, the transfer of the large-scale contradictions that pervade the Institutional Revolutionary Party (PRI).

New laboratories

The cultural foundations of Televisa and Rede Globo, far from being simple appendages of commercial projects, are powerful devices which bring them into the field of so-called formal education, and which allow these firms to enlarge their social functions considerably. It is easy to see

---

[2] See the bulletin published by Televisa during the "Second World Conference on Communication," organized by the group in July 1979, and the report presented by Televisa to the Mexican parliament in 1980 during the debates over the "right to information." On the history of radio and television in Mexico, see the special issue on "The state and television" of the journal *Nueva Politica,* Mexico, Vol. 1, no. 3, July–September, 1976.

the importance these non-traditional zones of influence assume for the introduction of new technologies and as laboratories for new forms of cultural action.

These so-called, philanthropic enterprises, excellent means of escaping income taxes, as we all know, are privileged establishments through which the state is willing to delegate some of the functions that are its responsibility to private enterprise. Through "Telecurso 2° Grau" (Telecourse, 2nd degree) of the Roberto Marinho Foundation, or through the university courses of the Televisa cultural foundation (6 hours a day) a new model for collaboration between the public and private sectors has been established. Moreover, this activity is a way of channeling state funds. (See *Boletin Intercom,* Sao Paolo, 1981, No. 32, p. 9.)

In 1978, the Roberto Marinho Foundation received the first prize of the Brazilian Association of Marketing for "merit in marketing." The commentaries accompanying the presentation of this prize speak for themselves.

> Profiting from the immense potential of television to contribute to the education of individuals, is a universal theme. Today, throughout the whole world, educators, researchers in social sciences, and psychologists are debating the influence of television and its role in the development of children, as well as the possibilities of transforming it into an efficient cultural instrument. The solutions suggested are extremely varied. There are countries which consider this activity as being part and parcel of the educational process of the state, and reserve for the state the right of exploitation on all channels. Others, The United States, for example, and some Latin American countries, confine television to the private sector, leaving the market to exercise its influence on the programing. No country appears, however, to have found the ideal formula. We are seeing, throughout the whole world, the creation of private stations where previously there were only government stations and second, the creation of educational channels which are creative competition between private and public channels. This coexistence does not appear to be a good solution either. The very small audience for the educational channels, apart from several important exceptions, means that the problems remain totally unresolved. In Brazil, however, we have inaugurated an imaginative formula that seems to constitute a solution unique in the world: to unite the efforts of educational television and private enterprise in order to place the technical and artistic resources of private television at the service of education, especially as our private television has attained a quality recognized the world over. One could ask why the Brazilian Association of Marketing wanted to award first prize to an initiative which, whatever its merits, does not correspond at all to marketing activity. The Association defined its line of action in 1978 in the following terms: "more products for a greater number of Brazilians." It feels that the duty of each community is to

contribute to the broadening of the internal market by creating new means which enable a greater and greater share of our population to participate in the economic life of our country. Tele-education fits into this perspective and has made an important contribution to it. (Quoted in TV Globo, 1980, pp. 27–28)

As skillful in marketing as in philanthropy, the Roberto Marinho foundation publishes and sells daily—the operation is called "multimedia"—the booklets of its television courses so that it can then—in another operation, called "Minerva"—broadcast these courses on the radio. A conglomerate like this one, which integrates horizontally all the means of distribution/broadcasting (including the videocassette), thus multiplies the same message by emitting it through several channels.

In Mexico, cable television was created in the 1960s by the Televisa monopoly. This new technology has allowed Televisa to overlap with the public sector (see Flores Salgado and Conde Luna, 1979). The so-called "social" system of cable television, experimentally installed in two poor suburbs in the interior and in the capital, offers courses in carpentry, masonry, plumbing and electricity. Gradually it is to incorporate into its programs courses of complete school programs. Here also, the Televisa cultural foundation is taking on the role of promoting new social uses for communication technologies.

It is interesting to note that cable television, exploitation of which by the private sector appears to be normal in numerous countries which consider it an extension of traditional television systems, gave rise in Brazil to polemics that emphasized the social and cultural scope of this technology. These diatribes culminated in 1979 in a parliamentary debate in Brazilia on the appropriateness of the installation of this new technology.[3] In the course of this debate, another, more serious problem was brought up—that of telematic networks.

---

[3] Already in 1974, the Brazilian Minister of Communications had refused the University of Rio Grande do Sul the authorization to go ahead with an experimental, cable distribution service project. Other groups were interested in setting up this type of service, among them Rede Globo. These proposals did not receive authorization, economic grounds (the excessive cost of importing material) being given as the reason for the refusal. During the parliamentary debate, opponents of the implantation of this new system advanced the argument that a service of this type could not be given solely to the private sector, but that universities should also be associated. A document which testifies to the concern of researchers, technicians, and university lecturers, demanded guarantees from the state that universities be authorized and even encouraged to exercise their social role and that public debate be instituted in order to preserve the collective interest.

They demanded an immediate slowing down of the introduction of cable television, given that the present conditions of installation implied "the abandoning to multinationals dominating the electronics industry with technology that the universities were perfectly capable of developing themselves." See the Brazilian Parliament (1979).

The dynamic of privatization

The partisans of the total privatization of television who seek to reduce the role of the state to a role of control and surveillance (as is the case for radio in most Latin American countries), are more and more numerous. This is true only in countries where television is still considered as public property; for in others, private exploitation began almost simultaneously with the advent of television.

The discussions which took place on this subject in Colombia are significant. Colombian television is provided under a mixed regime. The state owns all the channels but concedes hourly slots to private interests, which are obtained through invitations for applications, which are made every two or three years. The adjudicators or "programers" have to respect the policy and programming rules as defined by Inravision (National Radio and Television Institute), which supervises and controls the programs of the official networks that cover the country. Arguments in favor of the complete passage of television into the private sector, sometimes accompanied by subtle pressure (reduction of financial support), pivot curiously around a central theme: decentralization.

> Turning television over to the private sector would allow for a decentralization, local and regional channels thus being able to coexist. Both information and cultural and entertainment programs could benefit from the more direct contribution of the people and events in the region. The structure of private firms would allow for the interests of a city or zone to be better taken into account. At certain hours and for certain types of information, or for covering certain events, the collaboration of several regional channels can be imagined, either through a previous agreement, or through cooperation with different firms. (Yarce, 1980; see also Castro Caycedo, 1981)

In one form or another, the theme of decentralization is one of the poles of debate on the transformation of communications systems in Latin America.

In Peru, turning over television channels, nationalized under the government of General Velasco Alvarado to their former owners, has strengthened the monopolistic tendency of certain groups, such as the Delgado-Parker Group, owner of the firm Panamericana. Publishing houses, record companies, and sporting events all come under the activities of this group, present, like Televisa and Rede Globo, in numerous Latin American countries. This is all due to the new policy of the Peruvian state, based on private enterprise.

The system of cable television that the firm, Rexsa, has installed in Panama, is to provide direct reception via satellite and the enactment of videotex. The owners of the television channels in Panama, brought together, in effect, by this firm, continuously offer their audience several American channels. Also received by satellite are a, so-called, educational channel, which extends from opera to news, and a local news channel which gives meterological information, local news, etc. The brochure for subscribers states: "As programs come from English-speaking countries, most of the programs are in English, but we shall do our best to insert programs in Spanish as soon as they become available."

In 1980, the Argentine military junta decreed that the 66 radio and television stations, up until then administered by the state, should be turned over to the private sector. The first cable television network has laid down its circuits in the suburbs of Buenos Aires. The private owner of the system inaugurated another cable channel in 1982 with computer terminals, linked to a central computer for video games. But, as the director of this firm (Cablevisión) pointed out in 1981: "the equipment will also be linked to burglary and fire alarms, emergencies appearing immediately on screens in police or fire stations, indicating the address and other useful information" (Arveras, 1981).[4]

In Chile where the regime continues to be hostile to television in private hands, the Pinochet government granted in 1984 a franchise for the first cable television network in the country to a private group which also controls the conservative daily *El Mercurio*. There is no doubt that cable television projects are speeding up the process of privatization.

From psychological warfare to atomization through the market

In reality, in many Latin American countries, the more or less authoritarian control of society does not necessarily depend on the public or private character of the exploitation of communications systems. The different models are rather the result of history and particular circumstances.

To understand the underlying logic unifying apparently contradictory audiovisual systems, it is useful to introduce the theme of national security and its complement, pyschological warfare, both of which define an intellectual strategy that is found in very different countries. In countries where the guarantees of liberal democracy are not recognized by the state, the concepts of pyschological warfare and security have

---

[4] In November 1981, General E. Corrado, Under-Secretary for Communications, clarified the philosophy underlying the new telecommunications expansion plans: "Private initiative will be stimulated and facilitated in the sense of a uniting of efforts, so that we can go beyond the sterile controversies between 'privatization' and 'state control,'" (*Clarin* (science and technology section), November 3, 1981, p. 3).

lately become the main lines for the reorganization of communications and information systems. In the drawing up of new strategies, everything converges into the establishment of a consensus through fear, thus substantially modifying the old schemas of the liberal democratic state. An infinite number of forms of menace, which aim to make the restriction of individual liberties accepted, are making their appearance. National security—but also the security of each and everyone—is presented as a doctrine that will fill a vacuum in the life of the nation and of "threatened individuals." Psychological warfare is the operational framework in which, with its ups and downs, the dialectic between fear and security is developed.

The objectives of psychological warfare are defined in the following course of the Higher School of War of Brazil: "Psychological warfare is the planned employment of propaganda and the putting into practice of activities with a view to influencing the opinions, emotions, and behavior of hostile or neutral groups and obtaining their support for the success of "national goals." "Psychological action" is a part of this war, but it is destined for friendly sectors. It is defined as the whole of the resources and techniques used to create among individuals and collectivities the emotions, attitudes, predispositions, and behavior favorable to the obtaining of the required result." (Higher School of War, 1978; See also Mattelart, 1979c.)

Open psychological warfare against an internal enemy constitutes the first phase. It is characterized by the need for coercion when the plans of a new economic and social model are not yet viable and the first priority is to destroy the internal enemy. The second phase is more subtle in its objective, but also more structural. There is no irreversibility between the two phases, for the consensus that one hopes to establish through the voluntary acceptance of a social model creating security is predetermined in propaganda which marks out an enemy as the bearer of insecurity. It is thus always possible, faced with a new danger, to revert to open warfare. The new communications technologies in authoritarian states favor the growth of an illusion of liberty offered by the free competition of the market, whereas forms of social control are being strengthened. These forms remain hidden by appearances. Not only does the state not cede control but, through these forms, actually reinforces its concentration. The logic of control and the restriction of liberties underlies the model of restricted democracy that the state seeks to impose.

The initial moment of psychological warfare is by necessity voluntarist. A shop window in which to display the products of the new socioeconomic ordinance does not yet exist. The Brazilian definition, cited above, is more clearly behaviorist in inspiration. The market economy aspires, in turn, to reproduce a form of behavior initially imposed by force. The atomization of society, to which sheer physical repression has strongly contributed, is projected as a type of social and economic organization which gives preference to the free market. Exogenous propaganda thus seeks to transform itself into the hegemonic ideology of the everyday.

3. Telecommunications: A New Spatial Logic

Domestic satellites

In the 1960s and the beginning of the 1970s, discussion on the timeliness of launching regional or national communications satellites in Latin America invoked arguments linked to education. Thus was born the SACI-EXERN project in Brazil, led by the Institute of Space Research of San José dos Campos. The first stage unfolded in the North-East with the NASA satellite ATS 6. The experiment was stopped in 1977. The SERLA project, launched by the Andean Pact and conceived of for educational purposes, scarcely passed the stage of feasibility studies. In Colombia, the CAVISAT project, born in the shadows of certain U.S. universities like Stanford, which even anticipated giving out American diplomas to students resident in Latin America, fell through for lack of support (see Comuñicación y Cultura, 1975).[5]

Things have changed during the last few years. No one today thinks of looking at the field of education for reasons sufficiently worthwhile to justify the launching of satellites. Too many arguments have been advanced in opposition: pedagogical, economic, concern to preserve national and local cultural forms, etc. Telecommunications, on the other hand, seems to provide an irrefutable argument. The integration of national territory due to television, telephones, and later computer networks in the countryside, without forgetting transmissions between security forces on KU bands with mobile antennas, impose themselves as so many reasons beyond discussion. In transactions giving rise to the sale of national or regional satellites, the perspective through which manufacturers demonstrate the virtues of their produce has changed. Today's arguments aim to convince countries of the usefulness of owning their own satellites instead of having to rent channels on the Intelsat interna-

---

[5] On the Brazilian project, see McAnany and Oliveira (1980).

tional system. Satellite sellers emphasize: "The Intelsat treaty limits the the use of Intelsat transponders to public communications and forbids military and security uses. Moreover, the satellites are controlled by earth stations situated in other countries . . . The station which controls the national satellite is found in the same country. The government can thus use it at its convenience. The large number of terrestrial stations and the possibility of replacing them within hours makes the system virtually invulnerable to any act of sabotage." The supreme argument, advanced by French firms during the "Technical colloquium on new developments in telecommunications," held in Caracas at the end of March 1981 under the auspices of the French and Venezuelan governments, conceals a thinly veiled threat: "It is still possible to reserve a place on the geostationary orbit but this will be more difficult for future candidates."

In August 1980, Colombia announced its decision to launch its own satellite, thus affirming its right to the equatorial fringe disputed by the superpowers. Declared the Colombian Minister of Communications at the time: "Nothing is more important than using space because not only is it a resource limited in its expanse, but it probably will also be used by other countries, as is happening everywhere" (quoted by Alvarado, 1980, p. 3). The feasibility study for this satellite was carried out by the American firm COMSAT.

Brazil and Mexico have also announced the launching of national satellites for 1985. As for Argentina, it has announced an ambitious project of launching three satellites, which will cover the whole territory from North to South, and could constitute the world's biggest communication network within a single country. The Argentine plan fits into a long term plan that forecasts the production of its own satellites for 1990. To this end, the Government has decided to restructure the fighter plane factory at Cordoba in order to construct rocket engines there. Foreign firms are contributing some million of dollars to the project.

Latin America has been converted into a battlefield where many foreign corporations, especially American and French, confront one another. This battle sometimes gives rise to curious alliances between firms from different countries in order to check an opponent. In Colombia, for example, Hughes Aircraft (which has supplied 88% of the commercial satellites in use in the world) was in competition with the Franco-American consortium, linking Aerospatiale and Ford Aerospace Communications (*Business Week*, 1981b) before the present government postponed the project indefinitely in 1982. In Brazil, where once again, the alliance Aerospatiale-Ford was in competition with Hughes Aircraft allied in this case with the Canadian firm, Spar Aerospace, the government laid down negotiating conditions. The chosen firm had to guarantee, on the one hand, the transfer of its technology, and on the other, to propose advantageous commercial exchanges: three dollars of sales for every dollar imported. In spite of all expectations, Brasilia approved, in May 1982, the offer of Hughes-Spar for the manufacture of satellites. Aerospatiale had to be content with the launching by Ariane. Canada had apparently offered Brazil a better commercial return, notably in relation to the pulp and paper industry, as well as providing more favorable credit conditions.

As far as the development of space is concerned, the Brazilian project anticipates the production of second-generation satellites, seven years after the first, when the lifespan of the satellites soon to be launched into orbit will come to an end. The Institute of Space Research, which depends on the National Center for Scientific and Technological Development, is a key element in the project. From the beginning of the 1960s, it successfully set itself to work on the production of terrestrial reception instruments for spatial signals.

The deficiencies of the telephone network

Few people in Latin America imagine that the telephone, that familiar means of communication, has been called upon to abandon its modest function in order to become the basic element of the great computer networks which will characterize the computerized society of tomorrow.

Others know it only too well, and are furbishing up their economic and institutional tools to confront this approaching future. "If a country does not have a telecommunications system of good capacity and up-to-date technology, it cannot function as an efficient economy," declared the former director of telecommunications in Argentina and current President of COM/Citel, technical support arm of the OAS. An expert from the American consult firm, Arthur D. Little Inc., says that "all of Latin America, could end up by buying $18.6 billion worth of communications equipment over the next 10 years" (*Business Week*, 1981a). In their opinion, there is a tremendous lack of telephones in Latin America. Whereas there are only five telephones for every 100 people in Latin America (see Table 2.1), the average in the U.S. is nearly 77 telephones, and in Japan it is 51.

The hour for extensive invitations to tender for telephone systems seems to be striking once again. They should enable Latin America to pass from the analog to the digital era and, therefore, to be more able to absorb the global progress in computers. The telecommunications transnationals are to be found in all the projects for enlarging or modernizing networks: Philips, Plessey, Ericsson, ITT, Siemens, Thomson-CSF, Nippon-Electric, GTE. Some of these firms have controlled installations in

TABLE 2.1. TELECOMMUNICATIONS IN SOUTH AMERICA, 1980

Country	GNP/Head $US	Population (Millions)	No. of Telephones/100 Inhabitants
1. Venezuela	3,130	15.5	7.4
2. Surinam	2,360	0.4	13.4
3. Argentina	2,280	28.2	11.2
4. Uruguay	2,090	2.9	6.2
5. Brazil	1,690	121.4	7.1
6. Chile	1,690	11.1	5.4
7. Paraguay	1,060	3.3	2.1
8. Ecuador	1,050	8.2	2.8
9. Colombia	1,010	27.8	6.8
10. Peru	730	18.1	4.3
11. Guyana	570	0.8	2.1
12. Bolivia	550	5.5	1.8

Source: *Population Reference Bureau,* Washington; *AT&T Lines; Revista Nacional de Telecomunicações,* figures of Dec. 1980.

the majority of Western nations outside of the U.S. from the very beginning of the telephone (see Table 2.2).

This new boom is well illustrated by the case of Mexico. In 1981, the Mexican telephone company (Telefonos de Mexico) released its program of expansion for the national network. The objective was to multiply eightfold the number of lines presently in service (2.4 million) in the coming 20 years. Finances permitting, the plan should unfold in three stages: 563,000 supplementary lines in the period 1981–1986, 2.5 million between 1986–1990 and 13 million between 1990–2000.

The first phase, for which agreements have been concluded, aims at improving the urban network of Mexico City and the seven next biggest cities in the country. Nine firms made offers, but ITT and Ericsson, the two constructors installed in Mexico since the beginnings of the telephone, shared the 200 million-odd dollars of contracts between them. The Japanese, the Germans, the British, and the French were unable to get the better of the transnational American and Swedish groups, represented by their respective subsidiaries: Indetel and Teleindustria Ericsson.

To gain the agreement, both firms accepted two conditions stipulated by Telefonos de Mexico: a reduction of the foreign participation in their capital and an increased proportion of locally manufactured components in their production. Indetel, which obtained three-quarters of the market in the first phase of the program, decided to increase its overall capital, allowing the national bank, Somex, to increase its share from 18.8% to 40%. A second modification has brought Somex to 49% of the shares, level with ITT. Teleindustria Ericsson has followed the

TABLE 2.2. TOP TELECOMMUNICATIONS MANUFACTURERS, 1981

Rank	Companies	Revenues in Millions U.S. Dollars	% Telecom. in Total Revenues
1	WESTERN ELECTRIC (USA)	12 032.0	100
2	ITT (USA)	6 372.0	34
3	SIEMENS (GFR)	4 590.0	28
4	HITACHI (Japan)	3 179.2	20
5	LM ERICSSON (Sweden)	2 112.3	76
6	GTE (USA)	2 083.0	21
7	PHILIPS (Netherlands)	2 000.0	12
8	NEC (Japan)	1 735.0	36
9	CGE (France)	1 562.0	16
10	THOMSON-CSF (France)	1 518.0	31
11	NORTHERN TELECOM (Canada)	1 436.0	76
12	FUJITSU (Japan)	581.7	21
13	PLESSEY (U.K.)	560.1	40
14	OKI (Japan)	268.0	30
15	GENERAL DYNAMICS (USA)**	262.0	6

Source: Les Echos, 23 September 1982

*A division of the giant AT&T (American Telegraph and Telephone) which develops almost all of its activities on U.S. territory. In September 1982, AT&T and Philips announced the opening of talks with a view to joining their forces outside the U.S. to develop electronic telephone systems.

**Through its division, Stromberg-Carlson (partially bought up in 1982 by the British firm Plessey).

same path by ceding part of its shares to the financial institution, Nacional Financiera. Its capital is now shared between Ericsson (40%), Nacional Financiera (31%), and other Mexican investors (29%).

The two companies arc thus well-placed to continue to win future markets, at the price of an increased Mexicanization at the industrial and financial levels. Already, 90% of their production is of local origin, at least for receivers. The public authorities would like them to go further, but this appears difficult because it would require a transfer of advanced technology from the United States or Sweden. The solution envisaged is to mount a training program for Mexican technicians in Mexico and abroad in ITT and Ericsson factories.

The countries of the Andean Pact (Colombia, Venezuela, Ecuador, Peru, and Bolivia) are thinking of doubling the number of their lines between 1981 and 1985. According to the director of ASETA (Association of state telecommunications firms of the Andean sub-regional agreement), investment in these five years, "will be twice as big as all of the investment [we have] made in telecommunications since Samuel Morse" (*Business Week,* 1981a).

In Argentina, the national telephone firm awarded to Nippon Electric a big contract for an optical fiber network, called the "Digital Ring of Buenos-Aires." But the deficiency is enormous. In June 1981, the under-secretary of state for communications announced the installation of 200,000 telephone lines a year and admitted that the country needed 6 million lines instead of the current 2.5 million, most of which date back 30 or 35 years. From 1986, if Argentina wishes to attain a telephonic density in line with the planned development, it is estimated that 350,000 lines a year would have to be installed to meet the demand; this would require an investment on the order of 8,000 million dollars between now and the year 2000.

Japanese firms are also in the forefront in Peru. According to an agreement made in 1976, Peru receives continual aid from Japan in the field of telecommunications training, through Inictel (National Institute of Telecommunications Research and Training). Through this agreement, Japanese experts train Peruvian engineers and specialists, both civilian and military. The latter are working on the development of the first elements of a suitable technology in transmission and radio-broadcasting laboratories, equiped free of charge by Japan. In 1981, the firm Nippon Electric successfully bid for the installation of 150,000 new telephone lines.

As for Chile, it has preferred Israel and France. One of the new telephone firms installed in the country, Manquehue, promises 440,000 new telephone lines in the coming ten years. The equipment is to be supplied by Telrad Telecommunications and Electronic Industries Ltd, a firm based in Tel Aviv. The French firm Thomson successfully bid for an immediate working order to install another part of the telecommunications network joined to 27 electronic centers with a total of 153,000 lines.

France has thus not remained on the periphery of this battle for telephonic markets. It is also active in Argentina, Brazil, and above all in Venezuela, where it takes an active part in the development program for telephone services in the 6th Plan (1982–1985). The program, which anticipates 200,000 new connections a year, aims to increase the satisfaction of demand from 40% to 60% by 1983, and 72% by 1985. The primary objective is to assure access to telephone service to at least 38% of Venezuelan households. The Latin American market is so important to the administration of the French Postal and Telephone Services and to French businessmen that they decided to install a permanent "antenna" of French telecommunications for the whole continent in Caracas in 1982. This antenna, similar to one in Singapore for the Asian region, "will prolong isolated technical missions or purely commercial promotions through a permanent presence enabling a response, at any time, to the solicitations of local administrations by emphasizing the value of

French solutions in the field of telecommunications" (see Perrouin, 1982, p. 30).

The contradictions of equipment policy

The telephonic explosion in Latin America has not come about without conflict or tension, which often come from within the state apparatuses or from fluctuations in the priorities of the moment.

Brazil, which possessed about 6 million telephones in the 1970s, had decided to install between 900,000 and 1,000,000 telephones a year. It finally decided on a figure of 600,000 but installed only 350,000 in 1980, and forecast only 380,000 for 1981. One reason officially advanced to justify this reduction of investments was the priority accorded to oil supplies and hydroelectric stations. The projects for telephonic expansion were accompanied by measures aimed at stimulating national manufactures through mixed firms backed with Brazilian and foreign capital. (See Tables 2.3 and 2.4.)

Variations in priorities were to have a direct impact on these industries. In 1980, the Employers' Association of Brazil made it known that the telecommunications industry was only functioning at 55 to 60% of its capacity. Some firms of the sector had diminished their production or oriented it towards other domains. Such was the case of Ericsson which converted its casting presses for telephones into the manufacturing of cameras for Kodak, accessories for IBM, and horns for the automobile industry. Standard Electric, in its Rio de Janeiro factory, decreased its personnel from 7,700 to 3,200 at the beginning of 1980. The total of its operations declined in one year from 164 million dollars to 85 million dollars. The Japanese firm, NEC, went even further in the diversification of its activities, displaying a total absence of prejudice in its transnational alliances by allying with Sharp do Brasil in order to enter the agro-

TABLE 2.3. BRAZIL: TOP FOREIGN SUBSIDIARIES OF LOCAL MANUFACTURERS (1976: MILLIONS OF DOLLARS)

1. SA Philips do Brasil (Philips Group)	375.0*
2. Ericsson do Brasil Com. e. Ind SA (LM Ericsson)	351.5
3. Standard Eletrica SA (ITT)	155.7
4. Siemens SA (Siemens)	154.7
5. NEC do Brasil Electronica e Comunicações Ltda (NEC)	71.3
6. GTE Telecomunicacoes SA (GTE International Inc.)	51.3
7. Plessey ATE Telecomunicações Ltda (Plessey Co. Ltd.)	21.5

Source: *Communications Equipment and Systems*, Office of International Marketing, Bureau of International Commerce, US Dept. of Commerce, March 1978.
*Estimate

TABLE 2.4. BRAZIL'S TELECOMMUNICATIONS IMPORTS VS. EXPORTS (MILLIONS OF DOLLARS)

	1973	1973	1974	1975	1976
Imports	87.5	142.5	292.7	344.5	371.3
Exports	13.4	20.4	54.5	29.7	32.7

Relation of Equipment Imports to Total Imports
(Millions of Dollars)

	1972	1973	1974	1975	1976
Equipment Imports	43.2	58.0	60.9	40.9	99.1
Total Imports	87.5	142.1	292.7	344.5	371.3
Ratio	49%	41%	21%	12%	27%

Source: as for Table 2.3

food sector. In November 1981, after 53 years in the telephone industry, ITT abandoned the Brazilian market. The Japanese thus found themselves in first place, anticipating a wide opening of the Brazilian market.[6]

The process of technological modernization in telecommunications, of which the telephone constitutes one of the most important parts, is having a decisive effect on the redefinition of the different sectors that make up the state and in modifying the relations that the latter establishes with society as a whole. Telecommunications, which, not so long ago, were considered to be public services of limited range, today tend to take on an encompassing function within the new protocol of a country's data processing. The alliance of the telephone, the television, the computer, and the satellite as basic elements of telematic networks, breaks down the frontiers of a domain which, up until recently, came under the responsibility of various ministeries or bodies. The mention of official organizations, such as "Ministry of Transports and Communications"; "Superintendent of Electrical Services, Gas, and Telecommunications"; "Ministry of Transports, Communications and Tourism"; "General Administration of Electrical Factories and Telephones" shows the combination of other types of public service with telecommunications, as well as the purely technical character of the role attributed to it not so long ago.

---

[6] See Arjian (1979); see also the journal *Revista Nacional de Telecommunicações*, Sao Paulo, and *Business Week* (1981c).

4. Computers: Unequal Development

The measure of computer "progress"

What is the computer potential in Latin America in comparison with all of the Third World and the industrialized countries?

The Third World occupies only a tiny portion of the world market; generous estimations place it at between 5% and 7% of the total. Latin America, which already accounts for 60% of the mass media in the Third World, also includes those Third World countries with the highest level of computer development, even if this level remains weak compared to that of the industrialized countries.

A first indication, from the rare statistics existing, shows the extent of this gap. On the world market of computer and office equipment imports in 1978, Brazil, the most advanced Third World country in the information business occupied 16th place with 194 million dollars (Table 2.5). Mexico (20th), spent 161 million dollars, Argentina (24th), 100 million, and Venezuela (26th), 97 million. In comparison, the German Federal Republic, usually either first or else second behind the U.S., imported 1,875 million dollars of equipment and France, 1,531 million. Switzerland's imports were double those of Brazil. The only two African countries in the list of the first 50 were Algeria and Nigeria with 30 million each. The total computer imports in all of Africa (excepting South Africa) was half that of Switzerland. In the Far East, the most important importers were Hong Kong (180 million), South Korea (96), Singapore (61), the Phillipines (35), and Thailand (21). In the Middle East, Saudi Arabia occupied 29th place with 80 million, closely followed at the time by Iran. In 1980, the computer equipment imported by Saudi Arabia represented half the total in the Middle East. With several rare exceptions, these Third World nations are now classed as "newly industrialized countries."

A second indication comes from a survey on world computer re-

TABLE 2.5. 50 TOP COMPUTERS AND OFFICE EQUIPMENT IMPORT MARKETS (IN MILLIONS OF U.S. DOLLARS), 1977–1978*

Countries	1978		1977		% Change 1977–1978	% Change 1976–1977
	Rank	Imports	Rank	Imports		
Total	—	14,983.2	—		+ 28.2	+ 10.9
U.S.A.	1	1,961.5	2	1,369.8	+ 43.2	+ 15.9
West Germany	2	1,875.4	1	1,382.9	+ 35.6	+ 18.0
U.K.	3	1,533.1	4	1,159.8	+ 32.2	+ 18.6
France	4	1.531.3	3	1,335.4	+ 14.7	+ 11.3
Canada	5	787.4	5	669.5	+ 17.6	+ 10.2
Italy	6	782.1	6	620.0	+ 26.1	+ 8.7
The Netherlands	7	640.1	8	483.3	+ 32.4	+ 17.8
Japan	8	544.1	7	499.6	+ 8.9	+ 15.4
Belgium-Luxembourg	9	436.3	9	341.7	+ 27.7	+ 29.6
Switzerland	10	366.9	13	261.4	+ 40.3	+ 16.3
Sweden	11	362.5	10	302.7	+ 19.7	+ 15.2
Australia	12	361.9	11	281.7	+ 28.1	+ 21.7
Spain	13	296.2	12	273.9	+ 8.1	+ 7.8
Denmark	14	219.1	14	173.6	+ 26.2	+ 32.3
Austria	15	210.7	15	169.0	+ 24.6	+ 20.3
Brazil	16	193.7	17	135.2	+ 43.3	+ 0.9
Hong Kong	17	180.4	21	111.4	+ 61.9	+ 10.6
Ireland	18	175.3	16	156.8	+ 11.7	+ 66.1
South Africa	19	167.4	20	113.0	+ 48.1	+ 8.1
Mexico	20	160.8	22	106.8	+ 50.6	− 27.1
Soviet Union	21	152.8	18	115.6	+ 32.2	− 63.4
Norway	22	132.7	19	114.3	+ 16.1	+ 38.7
Czechosl.	23	113.5	25	82.7	+ 37.2	− 34.7
Argentina	24	99.8	26	81.0	+ 23.2	+107.1
Finland	25	99.8	24	88.6	+ 12.6	+ 4.9
Venezuela	26	97.2	23	89.3	+ 8.8	+ 28.6
Yugoslavia	27	96.9	27	76.2	+ 27.1	+ 62.5
South Korea	28	96.2	28	64.6	+ 48.9	+ 41.3
Saudi Arabia	29	80.1	36	39.0	+105.3	+ 51.2
Iran	30	63.3	33	44.2	+ 43.2	− 3.0
Singapore	31	61.3	30	49.9	+ 22.8	+ 24.7
Israel	32	58.7	35	41.6	+ 41.1	− 1.6
East Germany	33	57.3	31	49.1	+ 16.7	+ 14.7
Hungary	34	53.4	32	48.9	+ 9.2	− 37.3
Poland	35	49.8	29	53.0	− 6.0	− 62.3
Iraq	36	47.0	50	14.7	+219.7	+ 58.1
Portugal	37	45.8	37	35.9	+ 27.5	+ 42.5
New Zealand	38	41.1	34	42.2	− 2.6	− 0.7
Philippines	39	35.3	39	30.2	ǀ 16.8	− 1.6
Algeria	40	29.7	42	21.0	+ 41.4	+ 7.7

TABLE 2.5. (*Continued*)

Countries	1978		1977		% Change 1977–1978	% Change 1976–1977
	Rank	Imports	Rank	Imports		
Total	—	14,983.2	—		+ 28.2	+ 10.9
Greece	41	29.5	43	20.7	+ 42.5	+ 23.2
Nigeria	42	29.4	38	34.6	− 15.0	+ 38.9
Chile	43	26.7	45	19.5	+ 36.9	+ 65.3
Bulgaria	44	25.9	40	23.4	+ 10.6	− 46.9
Romania	45	24.7	47	16.5	+ 49.7	− 40.2
Panama	46	23.8	41	22.4	+ 6.2	+ 27.3
Colombia	47	21.6	46	18.0	+ 20.0	+ 71.4
Thailand	48	21.0	—	13.2	+ 59.1	—
China	49	20.9	—	7.9	+164.5	—
Kuwait	50	20.9	48	16.1	+ 29.8	+ 62.6

Source: *DATAMATION*, January 1981
*A striking absence from this list: India, in the grip of a policy of import restrictions as part of its strategy to construct a national computer industry. See on this subject J. M. Quatrepoint, "L'Inde ou les balbutiements d'une informatique sans IBM," *Le Monde*, 22 September 1982. See also J. H. Bennett and R. E. Kalman (eds.), *Computers in Developing Nations*, Amsterdam-New York, North Holland Publishing, 1981.

sources existing in 1981.[7] Computers in developing countries represented 5.7% of the world total in volume and 4.2% in value. Latin America (including the West Indies) accounted for 54% of the computer resources of the Third World compared to 5% for Africa, 10% for the Middle East and 30% for Asia and Oceania. Brazil, Mexico and Venezuela possessed 77% of the Latin American total (see Table 2.6).

It is not always easy to obtain precise data on the stock of computers in different Latin American countries. The journal of Colombian computer users remarks in its annual review of 1980: "The task is not easy, given the lack of information provided by firms or users. For carrying out of this inventory, the collaboration of the latter was indispensable. They had to fill out a form distributed throughout the country. The rate of response was extremely low. However, owing to the marvelous collaboration of manufacturing and supply firms, apart from IBM which has a worldwide policy of refusing to give any information whatsoever, we have been able to obtain figures, perhaps inexact, but no doubt fairly close to reality." The report cited earlier by an agency of Venezuelan consultants, carried out for the U.S. Commerce Department, remarked

---

[7] *IDC Survey* quoted by Delapierre and Zimmerman (1983).

TABLE 2.6. WORLD TOTAL OF COMPUTERS AS OF JANUARY 1981 (BY COUNTRY OR REGION)

Country or Region	Number of Systems	% of Total	Value (in $ U.S. Millions)	% of World Total	Average Value (in $ U.S. Millions)
U.S.A.	56,515	34.3	58,165	42.6	1,029
West Europe	45,976	27.9	38,676	28.3	841
Japan	24,311	14.7	15,365	11.2	643
Asia/Oceania	2,675	1.6	1,742	1.1	651
Latin America	5,453	3.3	3,108	2.3	570
(Brazil)	(2,482)	(1.5)	(1,569)	(1.1)	(632)
(Mexico)	(1,174)	(0.7)	(526)	(0.4)	(448)
(Venezuela)	(436)	(0.3)	(183)	(0.1)	(420)
Africa	505	0.3	275	0.2	547
South Africa	1,129	0.7	894	0.7	792
Middle East	765	0.5	596	0.4	779
U.S.S.R. and Eastern Europe	21,616	13.1	11,884	8.7	550
Others	5,945	3.6	5,975	4.4	1,005
Total (excl. U.S.A.)	108,375	65.7	78,515	57.4	724
World Total	164,890	100.0	136,680	100.0	829
Total DCs	9,398	5.7	5,721	4.2	609

Source: IDC survey

similarly in 1979: "It is to be regretted that of all the computer distributors consulted for this study, only IBM refused to cooperate."

Apart from countries like Brazil and Mexico, there exist very few official statistics. This situation is likely to change rapidly to the extent that national computer policies are instituted. With the same reservations as the Colombian association or the consultants in Caracas, we shall provide several figures demonstrating the presence of the big computer firms in the Latin American market. In Chile for example, IBM represents 56.8% of the total value of the installed stock and Burroughs 13%. In Venezuela, the same two companies control respectively 47.7% and 17.2% of the market. In Argentina, IBM represents 46.7% of the installed capacity, NCR 9.5%, Olivetti 8%, and the rest spread among a dozen companies. In Brazil, where Olivetti is the uncontested leader in small units, IBM represents 84.2% of the stock of large units. Invariably, therefore, IBM is the market leader, with Burroughs. NCR and sometimes, as in Mexico, Honeywell, far behind (Associación colombiana de usuarios de computadoras, 1980; *Mercado,* 1981; Informatica, 1979b; Final Report, 1980; SEI, 1981; Mexico Secretaria, 1980).

Various proposals have been made for measuring the development of computerization in different countries. Researchers from IBM and Mitsubishi Consulting Ltd. have perfected a classification defining the different stages through which each country must necessarily pass and enabling them to determine the level reached at any given time. Each stage is defined by eight key variables whose junctions allow one to situate a country through its evolution curve. These eight variables are: number and size of computers, state of teaching of data processing, applications of the computer, government use of computers, share of technology held by nationals, official policy towards computers, international assistance in computer technology, existence of professional data processing groups, and user associations. In turn, these variables are examined in respect to the role played by certain key institutions for the "transfer of computer technology" such as the government, universities, computer manufacturers, transnational corporations, United Nations agencies, and other foreign organizations for technical cooperation and assistance.

According to these researchers, seven stages can be defined. The *initial stage* corresponds to a situation of initial introduction or experimentation (for example, Haiti). The *initial to basic stage* is characterized by the beginning of use and knowledge of the technology (Honduras, Bolivia, Ecuador, Paraguay, Dominican Republic, El Salvador, Guatemala, Costa Rica, and Guyana). The *basic stage* is marked by the proliferation of machines and installations (Peru, Chile, Colombia, Uruguay, Cuba, and Panama). The *basic to operational stage* implies the reconsideration of the fundamental problems of the impact of computerized activities on the national balance of payments, government activities, and the life of firms (Venezuela, Puerto Rico). The *operational stage* is described as a consolidation stage (Mexico, Argentina). The *operational to advanced stage* begins with the integration of the various elements of the data processing industry into a national framework (Brazil). The seventh stage is the *advanced stage*, which corresponds to the ultimate level of maturity; it has not been attained by any Latin American country.

Only an indicative value

The classification of Latin American countries according to the above typologies was carried out by Ramon C. Barquin and other researchers in 1976 (Barquin et al., 1976). But as a Chilean specialist, commenting on a conference in United Kingdom in 1980, pointed out:

> The classifications often rest on outdated data. I believe this to be the case in the classification of Chile in the basic stage of computer development. It is obvious that Chile has gone beyond this phase, if we accept the

definition. What, therefore, is our level? The operational level is defined as 'when a widespread understanding of computers exists' in government and private decision-making circles, along with the use of large machines, and the existence of training and several specialists of excellent quality. We create and produce software and manufacture a little hardware. Computers affect many disciplines, particularly those of science' medicine, and engineering. At the conference, the cases of Brazil, Hong Kong, India, and Mexico were cited as illustrations of this stage. Moreover, there is another intermediary stage between basic and operational which includes Egypt, South Korea, Thailand, and Venezuela. In my opinion, several of the characteristics defining the operational stage are fully realized in Chile. Several large-scale computers, training software, and impact in other domains are all to be found. Admittedly, in so far as hardware is concerned Chile does not "manufacture," although the technical capacity to manufacture certain components does exist. In this respect, there is obviously no possible comparison with Brazil where a computer industry already exists. (Pino, 1980, p. 17)

Another descriptive model has been developed at the Massachusetts Institute of Technology. It attempts to establish a potential index of the development of the computer industry. The Computer Industry Development Potential (CIDP) is composed of eleven weighted variables grouped under three headings. Economic variables include: a) Gross National Product (30 pts.); b) Per Capita GNP (15 pts.); c) Growth rates of GNP and per capita GNP combined (5 pts.); d) % of GNP in "high technology areas" (10 pts.). The educational variables are: a) literacy rate (10 pts.); b) relative number of students enrolled in secondary school or above (5 pts.); c) level of technical education (5 pts.). Finally, the technological variables are: a) Electricity generated (8 pts.); b) Number of telephones per 1000 (7 pts.); c) Number of television sets installed (2 pts.); d) Number of computers in the country (3 pts.).

IBM and Mitsubishi have proposed a correlation model between their stages of data processing development and the CIDP index. According to the results obtained by this model, the most advanced stage is equivalent to 65 points on the CIDP index (out of a total of 100). Brazil, the most advanced country in Latin America attained only 52 points in 1976.

These methods of classification have only an indicative value. It goes without saying that this type of typology and statistical analysis is based on the ideas of development and social progress which gives impetus to the model of expansion of industrial capitalism. More and more, this conception of progress and well-being is being called into question by groups demanding new forms of technology, more adapted to an alternative idea of development and to alternative social and cultural perspectives.

The transfer of a model of consumption

The first computer in Latin America was installed in the Venezuelan offices of the Creole Petroleum Corporation, which became a launching pad for computer development. In Central America, United Brands, which had previously installed the railway network uniting internal plantations with ports, became the pioneer of computer "modernization." Today, it is the fourth largest international record carrier, its subsidiary, TRT Telecommunications, coming behind the three biggest: RCA Global Communications, ITT World Communications, and Western Union International (a subsidiary of Xerox). Occidental Petroleum has installed the most advanced systems of communication in Peru so as to be linked to the world network of information.

These are, without a doubt, borderline cases, but paradigmatic ones all the same: the beginnings of computer technology in Latin America—as had been the case in other areas of communication and technology—corresponded to the needs of a development model founded on the interests of foreign firms and the monopolist concentration of capital.

A document presented by Brazil to the Fourth Conference of Latin American Computer Authorities (CALAI) sums up the phenomenon very well:

> Brazil, like many Latin American countries, entered the computer industry as a consumer of imported goods and services, whereas the central countries, particularly the United States, had already sufficiently developed their own markets and were seeking to conquer new markets owing to the opening up of new commercial frontiers in this sector. We learned how to handle the computer through courses, offered principally by hardware manufacturers who were both distributors and suppliers of material, owners of technology, and responsible for the training of specialized labor. Consequently, the first truly national firms created in our country devoted themselves to the performance of data processing and the development of applications, using software as a support base and importing the equipment. The function of the knowledge disseminated was to broaden the market and was limited to the technology of using computer resources which became veritable black boxes.

These analyses and diagnoses which indicate the extent of foreign dependence are doubtless correct, but they are surely insufficient. To limit oneself to them boils down to endorsing an overly unilateral and non-dialectical vision of the unequal relations linking the Latin American countries to the United States. One must, therefore, complete these analyses by an examination of the role played by national actors in the construction of a computerization model.

Chapter 3

How Computers Penetrate States

1. Detour Through the Recent History of European Countries

Return to national particularities: the meaning of an approach

One had to wait for the boom in the new phase in the expansion of telecommunications networks to see the crumbling of the McLuhanian idea of the "global village" which had dominated marketing clichés of the previous phase of mass communications expansion, particularly that of television. References to the specific nature of communication and information systems on each continent, or even each country, are appearing among those who had abandoned specific histories in favor of transnational cosmopolitanism. This phenomena is particularly visible today in Europe, but is also perceptible, with its own characteristics, in Latin America.

Let us look at the European case in a little more detail.

> Of all the technical aspects in setting up international dp installations, the biggest differences in operations are in the area of telecommunications... It drives multinationals wild to discover that what is legal in France may be illegal in Belgium and, while not banned, unavailable in The Netherlands. (*Datamation,* 1980)

Or again:

> There is no simple way to determine why some vendors—either European or American—are more active in pioneering new markets. America represents a more or less homogeneous market with a common language, constitution, and operating practices. In contrast, Europe comprises many countries differentiated not only by language but also by business customs, legislation, and constitutional structure. To operate successfully in Europe, a multinational must cope with a wide range of economic situations. (*Datamation,* 1981b)

These are observations by specialists of telematic systems in the magazine *Datamation:* "American methods," which have been used until recently by the big American telecommunications firms to tackle the European market, pose more and more problems (see also *Datamation,* 1981a).

> On the eastern side of the "pond," telecommunications services are, without exception, provided by a monopoly regime. Ah, you might say, sounds just like AT&T. The de facto monopoly of the Bell system is markedly different—especially since the FCC gave the go-ahead to value-added networks. By way of contrast, telecommunications services are provided exclusively by government departments described generically as PTTs (European Post Offices), administrations owned by publicly held corporations, such as the UK Post Office. The nature and expense of these monopolies is severe at best. (*Datamation,* 1980).

This same view of the difficulties met by industrial actors in the search for macrosocial uses for telecommunication systems, can be found, almost word-for-word, among exporters of mini- and microcomputers. The social uses imagined by manufacturers of these microelectronic products in terms of U.S. experience, does not necessarily correspond to the expectations of Europeans (nor, as we shall see later, to those of Latin Americans). The hobby market, which initially helped the breakthrough of the personal computer in the United States, does not arouse the same interest in Europe. In this area, Great Britain is the exception that confirms the rule. The American firms which dominate the market (Apple, Commodore, Tandy-Radio Shack) and the Japanese firm Sharp have had to reorient their strategies. Their directors state forthrightly: "The American manufacturers are beefing up their European marketing efforts by trying to become more European—tailoring programs, models, and instruction manuals to local tastes. Commodore, for example, has founded a separate European software group to write programs for basic applications like bookkeeping and word processing. Apple is beginning to develop software and manuals for European users." As the director of Apple Computer International recognised: "Until now, everything was essentially American designed . . . Now, as the markets have got larger, we'll move toward more European products" (*Business Week* International Edition, June 15, 1980, p. 99).

The battle is only beginning; the market was estimated at a thousand million dollars in 1981, in other words, a little more than half of the American market. In 1980, shipments for all of Europe increased by 80%, reaching 140,000 microcomputers. In 1983, according to these firms' forecasts, this figure would have tripled, and the market would be worth two thousand million dollars. The most developed market is that of the German Federal Republic; at the beginning of 1980, the stock of desktop computers barely reached 10,000 units, but 18 months later, it exceeded 50,000.

The stakes are considerable. The European firms, which lost the market for large mainframe computers in the 1960s to IBM and Honeywell, and, in the 1970s, a large part of the minicomputer market to Digital Equipment and Data General, want to conquer, at the least, 65% of the market for small business computers. In effect, it is this business use which seems to have carried the day throughout Europe. In 1981, business uses represented 62% of the market, compared to 20% for scientific uses, 10% for educational uses, and only 8% for hobbies or pastime uses. According to forecasts, the personal computer will have to become much more popular before becoming a "mass phenomenon" in Europe.

There is nothing astonishing in this return to the national characteristics of communication and information systems. This trend, however, is in dialectical relation to the powerful movement toward the internationalization of local economies in which networks owned by nation-states are regularly transformed into transnational networks. For the first time, applications of the technological alliance between telecommunications, computers, and audiovisual equipment are spreading through the whole of society. Spearheads of the modernization of institutional systems and the production process—some prefer to speak of a mutation, thus suggesting the change in the nature of the societies affected—these technologies are laying bare the structural foundations of the countries in which they are being inserted.

By indicating the particular paths followed in the process of computerization in each society, we are also able to carry out an in-depth analysis of each of those societies, for the process of computerization of a society does not take place uniformly. The different sectors of the state, civil society, and the economy all submit to it at different times. A telematic tidal wave does not exist. There are parallel processes or convergents which carry each society towards overall computerization. There are, however, both vanguards and rearguards in this advance wave. There may also be sectors that are not necessarily in agreement with the general orientation of the computerization process. These are the elements which the top management of transnational corporations is taking account of in confused fashion when, in their own words, they make allowances for the resistances, checks, obstacles, and alliances that they meet in their strategy of market penetration.

Recent lessons

A globalizing view of the computerization process is incapable of taking into account the widely different situations in which various countries find themselves when they are faced with new communications and information technologies and by the directions in which, what industrial firms call "computer demands or needs," are formulated and developed.

The history of computer applications in European countries is a recent one, yet, nevertheless, for those who know how to analyze it, what has happened in each country yields useful information for other, less advanced countries. It allows other questions to be raised in connection with the following central question: What are the basic operators in the penetration of the computer into the social fabric? Some examples:

• The preference for minicomputers in the Federal Republic of Germany cannot be explained without looking at the political structure of the country, little inclined towards centralization, at least in civil affairs. Marginal to this observation is the fact that one cannot trace the history of computer applications in the Federal Republic of Germany without noticing the extreme rapidity with which, under pretext of combating terrorism, the police system furnished itself with the most sophisticated equipment to be used for identifying and maintaining files of suspects. Along with Northern Ireland, the Federal Republic is undoubtedly the European country that best exhibits the repressive uses of the new electronic machines. What we need to know here is the effect of the computerization of this sector of government on the state as a whole and on the production of electronic equipment and computers by German firms. One might recall, for example, that by 1977, the firm, Nixdorf, had developed the most highly perfected police information system in the world in Berlin? (See *Computer Decisions*, February, 1977, p. 26.)

• The importance of a continuing centralizing heritage in France can be seen, first of all, in the development of a market oriented towards big mainframe computers. In order to reverse this tendency, the French government has actively encouraged the minicomputer industry through its telecommunications policy. Whereas the German Federal Post Office refuses to encourage data transmission by lowering its tariffs, the French government has reduced them to favor the growth of distributed processing systems.

• The infrastructure adopted in its computerization by the banking sector, well-known for its pioneering character in the expansion of uses for the computer in many European countries, provides another type of example. In Great Britain, the five largest banks concentrate most of the banking computer infrastructure of the country and control very large networks that supply the centralized data processing systems. In contrast, in Federal Germany, the top four banks (in terms of assets) represent only a small portion of the total market. Each bank has a relatively small computer department, thus fitting in with the pattern of a fragmented market (*Datamation*, 1981b).

• Computerization in the Scandinavian countries furnishes yet another illustration. This computerization was denounced as being often excessive by a report, *Privacy and Vulnerability,* which pointed out that unneccesary computerization in Sweden has led to an excessive dependence on computers in national activities that in the case of a catastrophe, no more than 14% of Swedish firms or other computer-equipped institutions could continue to run manually. The boom in computers in Sweden goes back to about 1945, when the state, on the initiative of military circles, launched a national program aimed at equipping public agencies, including the national administration and both military and civil research agencies with an electronic calculator, as soon as possible. In 1953 these efforts led to the perfecting of a calculator, considered at the time to be the fastest in the world, named BESK (abbreviation for Binary sequence electronic calculator).

In 1956, this project was taken up by the firm, Atvidaberg Industrier, whose corporate name has since been changed to Facit. Not only the research team, but also the computer hardware were integrated into the firm. Consequently, this date marks the end of the innovative action by the public authorities to develop Swedish computers (Lindeborg, 1982, pp. 2–3). In 1970, when computers were used in the general census, debates began on the subject of computer privacy. In 1973, Sweden passed the first law in the world on computers and privacy.

Whereas banks in many countries have yet to begin to install terminals to facilitate their accounting, Scandinavian banks are modernizing their networks for the second or third time. The same observation can be made for savings accounts. Local administrations have not been left out in the process of computerization. Organizations have been established which supply central and regional computing facilities. In Denmark, for example, Kommunedata makes it possible for nearly every town in the country to have on-line access to files of all kinds: population registers, budgetary data, education and health information, etc. Whereas in France, which remains strongly agricultural, it was only in 1982 that timid telematic experiments were carried out with farmers from the South. The Danish Agricultural Council has long since developed a central on-line system for farmers. The system handles business applications, feed optimization analysis, pricing data, etc. Agricultural inspectors carry portable terminals when making their rounds of farms, feeding back information into the center by phone/modem links (*Datamation,* 1981c).

The penetration of the new technologies into production processes is another indication of its importance, particularly in Sweden. For 16,000 white collar employees at its headquarters in Göteborg, the car manufacturer, Volvo, has 4,000 to 5,000 terminals. The parts division has one terminal for every three employees while the truck division has one for every five. Volvo is in the forefront of automatization and Sweden as a whole had the biggest number of industrial robots in relation to its labour force (8 per 1000 workers) in 1980.

In spite of the presence of IBM, which dominates 60–70% of the total stock of computers in Scandinavian countries, Ericsson in Sweden continues to be one of the five biggest telecommunications companies in the world (more than 78% of Ericsson's sales come from the international market). The case of Sweden raises a question. Why have certain countries with a limited domestic market succeeded in maintaining electronic hardware firms on the international market which are in a position to compete with the Americans and the Japanese? The history of Ericsson and also that of the Dutch firm, Philips, would be very informative in this respect.

Swift country

Our last example, Belgium, which also appears to be far removed from Latin America, is, in fact, closely related through the transnational networks which originate in Brussels.

If one were to retrace the history of the process of computerization in this little European country and examine the first application of the computer on a significant scale, it would no doubt be necessary to look closely into what constitutes the backbone of its economic power today: the banking and financial sector and the "agro-chemical" macro-network, an industrial specialization which has succeeded in working its way into the new international division of labor (see *Futuribles*, 1980). We should not, however, forget the role of NATO, which has propelled Belgium into a parallel development through modernization of some of its telecommunications services. This development is little known, primarily because it is the direct concern of the Allied staff commands and their security strategies. Here, we refer to the systems of satellite communication which, although never revealed in public, must have provided the model for computer development in the country. In 1975, NATO had entered into its third phase of satellite communication as an essential part of the defense system for the Western world, and were much more advanced at the time than civil applications of this space technology (see Mattelart, 1979b, pp. 100–101).

Today the banking sector attracts the most attention, doubtless because it was one of the economic sectors where computerization began, for the most part before the advent of the present crisis. In 1981, Belgian unions estimated that the introduction of microelectronics in the banking sector would affect 70% of the staff; the operations and transfers sector would undergo a reduction of work on the order of 75%, the typing and secretarial sector 30% and the accounting and exchange sector 30%. Another indication of its effect is that in the banking and insurance sectors, employment increased from 72,000 to 190,000 between 1964 and 1974, while from 1974 to 1977, the number of jobs remained almost stationary (190,000 to 194,000), even though the number of transactions increased. It must be pointed out, however, that Belgium suffers from a situation of "overbanking." It has become the country with the highest number of banking branches based on population.

The history of the computerization of Belgian banks is a part of the history of the concentration and internationalization of the economy which has taken place, particularly in the last fifteen years. This concentration can be seen in the reduction of Belgian banking firms: 59 in 1978 as against 73 in 1965. Internationalization is revealed by, among other things, the massive implantation of foreign banks, which bring with them transnational corporations: 49 foreign banks in 1977 compared to 14 in 1972. This internationalization is also visible in the internationalization of credit schemes, which can be seen, for example, on the financial Euromarkets. Belgian banks are to be found more and more alongside the big partners of transnational banks on the European bond market. At the end of 1970, the share of transactions in currency exchange already represented more than a third of the total balance sheet and reached 42% by 1978. By the end of the same year, nonresident assets represented 45.2% of the total balance sheet of Belgian currency, compared to 37.5% at the end of 1970.

The history of this internationalization is one of ebbs and flows. The recession and redeployment of the last few years have followed the growth and expansion of transnationals in the 1960s and early 1970s. Because of its splendid period during the "golden sixties," Belgium has become an international banking center. Symbolically, Brussels was chosen as the pivot of the SWIFT network (Society for Worldwide Interbank Telecommunications). (See Figure 3.1.) Inaugurated in May 1973, this network is the biggest in the world for the transmission of payment orders and other international transactions, such as verifying the solvency of credit cards and related matters. By 1980, 683 banks throughout 26 countries were integrated into this network and the volume of messages transmitted reached an average of 180,000 a day. In 1982, this average had reached 400,000.

The origin of SWIFT (a cooperative, non-profit firm legally registered in Belgium) dates back to 1969 when a small group of European banks took the initiative for developing a system of interconnections for the exchange of messages. In 1971, 69 European and American banks joined together to entrust the construction of the SWIFT network to the

FIGURE 3.1. SWIFT

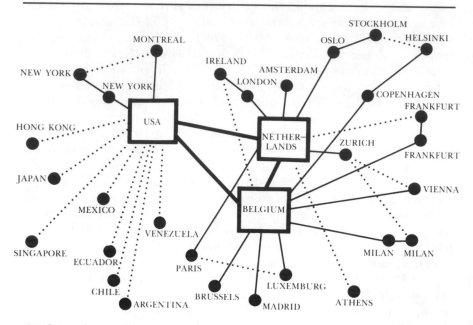

■ Operating Centre
  (Burroughs Dual B4800)
● National Processor
  (Burroughs Dual B775/B875)
— Primary Circuit
  (9600 BPS Full Duplex)
... Back-up Circuit
  (9600 BPS Full Duplex)

American firm, Burroughs. In 1973, SWIFT began with a membership list for 240 banks. Each bank is furnished with a computer terminal called SID (SWIFT Interface Device), a medium sized or minicomputer especially conceived to act as a vehicle for the software required by the SWIFT network. Long responsible for linking, almost exclusively, the big European and American banks, the network has recently broadened in scope to take in the Far East and Latin America, thus manifesting the shifting of the world economy towards the newly-industrialized countries. Curiously enough, this is one of the only data transmission networks not to be affected by the efforts of certain countries to restrict the free, transnational flow of information. Equipped only with systems approved by SWIFT (the systems manufactured by Burroughs, General Automation, and ICL), this network chooses its president from among the senior management of the big transnational banks; currently its Deputy Chairman comes from Chemical Bank.

With the partial withdrawal of transnationals from the European continent, some foreign banks have also withdrawn, while others that have remained in Belgium have simplified their structures. Citibank, for example, suppressed its agency network and reduced its branch personnel by nearly 40% toward the end of the 1970s. American Express acted similarly by laying off more than half its staff between 1974 and 1980. At the same time, these big banks have changed their target-clientele. They are trying to do away with operations which concern clients of modest means (by diminution of less profitable services such as credit transfers and checks) and are seeking a clientele whose operations correspond to the highly profitable transactions of the transnational structure.

As much in foreign-owned banks as in Belgian ones, the acceleration of computer applications has contributed to staff compression in the name of productivity. Some, not content to computerize their own business, have begun to offer the services of their computer department to other firms. In its strategy of transnational diversification (it draws more than 65% of its income from other countries), the Citibank has created a group of financial and information services which, in 1979, reported a net income of 541 million dollars (*Business Week,* 1980). The computer services offered by these banks has come to fill a growing need for assistance for future users of the computer. They advise users on computer applications, hardware and software choices, and the integration of the system into the firm, as well as sometimes providing training and putting their own telematic network at the disposal of these new users. The large European banks have also invested in service firms.

The wave of the implantation of new foreign banks is, admittedly, over. Still, the role of Belgium as a financial turntable for the transnational economy has been confirmed little by little, even if other centers are emerging as illustrated by the new ramifications of the expansion of the SWIFT network towards the Far-East (Lloyd and Peltu, 1981).

Because of the great impact of microelectronics on employment, the banking sector is undoubtedly the one, that in the analysis by the Belgian unions, attracts the most attention. More often than not, it is the executives and trade union militants from the banking, insurance, and savings sector who have played a pioneering role in Belgium, along with printing workers, in raising discussion on the socioeconomic and cultural effects of computers to the level of a central preoccupation for the entire union movement. This tends to show that the level of consciousness on the "stake of computers" is far from being homogenous in the working classes and that they are responding to concrete struggles based on, among other things, the evolution in work conditions.

Unfortunately, there are few studies that allow us to reply to the numerous questions raised by these examples of the different processes of computerization in European societies.

In the world panorama, using Europe to open the topic, where do the various Latin American countries stand? What are the elements within these countries that will match the model as these countries move towards computerization?

To draw up an inventory of the sectors which have taken the initiative in computerized "modernization" is, in fact, to pinpoint the forces remodeling society and its institutions in each country. The differentiated, asynchronous process of computerization is generally accompanied by tensions between different parts of the state, between the state and certain social groups, and, indeed, between different sectors of society. The new information technologies are creating fissures within the state apparatus, through which are conveyed not only the contradictions, but also the convergences between civil and military agencies, between private and public groups, between technocrats and technicians, between international and national capital, and between authoritarian and democratic conceptions of the rights of individuals and nations.

2. The Unbalanced State

A model of popular participation?

On the luminous screen of a computer terminal at the income tax department of Panama, one can read a list of the 200 largest taxpayers of the country and know immediately who is not up to date with their payments. This fact takes on importance when one realizes that these 200 people's taxes represent 75% of the total tax receipts and constitute the essential part of state revenue.

In 1960, the Panamanian government installed the first computerized tax control system. It continues to be improved, assuring correct payments on external sales (called rent taxes) and internal sales (taxes on the transfer of movable goods). The particularities of the Panamanian economy explain the crucial importance of this administrative apparatus for tax payments. The Panamanian economy depends, totally, on the commercial transactions carried out in the free zone of Colon, the vast commercial zone of Panama City, and on the revenue from the canal.

The modes of administering the national budget define the political functioning of Panamanian society. Thus, the Contraloria General (a sort of court of revenue) has launched a project of popular control over public spending, unique at least in this part of the world, if not elsewhere. The Revenue Court, which constitutes a veritable state within a state in the organization chart of the Panamanian government, was inspired by the Cybersyn project, launched in Chile under the Popular Unity government. Relying on the support of the CORFO (Corporación de Fomento, i.e., Corporation for the encouragement of development), which was responsible for the administration of public enterprises, the Cybersyn project attempted to develop and apply modern cybernetic policies to the planning of the economy, particularly in the nationalized sector. According to one of the principals on the Chilean project:

> The central point of view of Cybersyn is entirely in its name, a contraction of cybernetic and synergy. Here, cybernetic means considering a sys-

tem as a totality with a structure, dynamic and relation between control, information, planning, and decision. The concept of synergy underlines the fact that efficiency and return do not result from abstract, formal controls imposed from outside, but on the contrary, are linked to the multiplying effect engendered by the relations of cooperation between the different elements of the system.[1]

The Cybersyn project used a telex network operating in real time, which communicated the essential data, allowing the measurement of performance variables of firms in the nationalized sector. The data was processed by a central computer, thanks to specially developed programs. The project also possessed carefully-analysed basic elements which, when necessary, enabled quick decisions to be made concerning corrections of the conjuncture or strategic planning. With its limited means, the project tried to realize a decentralized computer scheme, which sought to assure workers' participation in the control centers, in the planning and management of this nationalized sector of the economy.

The Panamanian Revenue Court project takes the idea of an operational decentralization with a central control-point and is extending it to the whole of the government, defined as a functional unity. Decentralization is conceived of as sector-based, regional planning used in the search for solutions for local problems whose sum constitutes national problems. The aim is for decentralization of planning and decentralization of execution, but without losing the central control of information. This is what government authorities call "decentralized centralism."

This fundamental idea is translated physically in a computer installed in the premises of "Contraloria," where a teleprocessing system is in permanent communication with offices in the regions and localities through the terminal screens of the system. The project proposes, in fact, a restructuring of the state's operation, for this new system of accounting will facilitate planning, execution and control as well as sup-

---

[1] Cf., the compilation of F. de Cindio and C. de Michelis (1980). This compilation includes texts by Stafford Beer, Raul Espejo, Mario Grandi, and Herman Schwember. Under the Popular Unity regime, the text "Fanfare for Effective Freedom" by Stafford Beer, the British cybernetician and adviser to the Cybersyn project, was published in Spanish under the title, "Practica cibernética en el gobierno." This text was presented to the Third Richard Goodman commemorative conference at the Polytechnic of Brighton on 14 February 1973. This Chilean experiment, which had the merit of bringing together, in one project, political leaders, trade unionists, and technicians, has not yet resulted in sufficiently ample ideological debate on the problematic relations between science, technique, and democracy. The use of "systems theory" by this project needs more profound discussion. Some elements for such a discussion can be found in journals of critical scientists, notably, *Science for the People* and the *Radical Science Journal*.

ply accurate information, thus enabling better economic management by the authorities. With its computer, the Revenue Court becomes the depository of the financial information of the government, transforming into a data bank for multi-institutional use.

The project envisages the possibility of establishing popular control over the administration of the budget. Control would be exercised through a network of terminals installed in each community—the smallest administrative division of the country—and in all types of the most significant local community groups. Each terminal would supply, in real time, information on the overall state and allocations of the budget.

As the project started it provoked different reactions on the part of certain administrative sectors, which is commented on in the following opinion by a high-ranking civil servant from the Revenue Court: "The success of this project depends on a change in the attitudes of civil servants who have to lose the spirit of traditional compartmentalization to open themselves to a wider and more human conception of the goals of the state" (Contraloria general de la República, 1980).

While its focus is welcome, the Panamanian project exhibits some flaws. Seduced by the cybernetic approach to the state as a "system," these public servants leave little place for an analysis of the relations between the state and the various components of civil society. The "social" aspect of society appears more as an added value. This absence of questioning of the popular organization and the decentralization of power, which appear in this project as "transparent" notions, that is, expurgated of their social contradictions, evidently cannot be explained without reference to the populist character of the regime set up by General Omar Torrijos, who was killed in a suspicious plane crash at the end of 1981. However, in spite of these structural limitations, the plan for the Panamanian Court of Revenue is one of the most original of the subcontinent.

Computerization of an oil country

The collection of taxes in Panama, the veritable vertebral column of the country's economy, has an equivalent in Venezuela: oil. By nationalizing the oil industry in 1975, Venezuela inherited a gigantic computerized enclave. From the 1950s on, the oil industry, in the hands of big transnationals, had begun to install computers, as much to resolve technological and operational problems as to improve administrative management.

Nationalization in 1975 did not change the existing network of international connections imposed by a centrifugal model of data processing. Nor did it change its dependence in respect to IBM. The Venezuelan oil industry had access, thanks to the Telenet data transmission network (see Chapter 4), to four specialized foreign data banks: three American

TABLE 3.1. VENEZUELA: IMPORTS OF COMPUTERS AND RELATED EQUIPMENT BY MAJOR SUBCATEGORIES AND COUNTRY OF ORIGIN, 1976, 1977, 1978 AND 1983 (U.S. DOLLARS IN THOUSANDS)

Country	1976 $	1976 Share	1977 $	1977 Share	1978 $	1978 Share	1983* $	1983* Share
I. Mini Computers								
U.S.A.	2,600	50.5	3,800	62.3	12,300	76.9	14,300	65.0
W. Germany	400	7.8	600	9.8	800	5.0		
Canada	300	5.8	400	6.6	400	2.5		
Other	1,850	35.9	1,300	21.3	2,500	15.6		
Total	5,150	100.0	6,100	100.0	16,000	100.0	22,000	100.0
II. Small, Medium, Large Computer Systems								
U.S.A	13,100	55.9	13,100	67.6	21,300	71.5	26,600	70.0
W. Germany	650	2.8	800	4.1	900	3.0		
Brazil	700	3.0	900	4.6	2,700	9.1		
Canada	1,400	6.0	1,200	6.2	500	1.7		
Japan	5,600	23.8	2,000	10.3	1,600	5.4		
Other	2,000	8.5	1,400	7.2	2,800	9.3		
Total	23,450	100.0	19,400	100.0	29,800	100.0	38,000	100.0

III. Peripherals (Separately Imported)

	Value	%	Value	%	Value	%	Value	%
U.S.A.	400	17.5	500	20.0	2,500	50.0	5,100	60.0
Brazil	200	8.7	500	20.0	800	16.0		
Canada	300	13.0	600	24.0	600	12.0		
Japan	1,300	56.5	700	28.0	600	12.0		
Other	100	4.3	200	8.0	500	10.0		
Total	2,300	100.0	2,500	100.0	5,000	100.0	8,500	100.0

IV. Data Communications Equipment

	Value	%	Value	%	Value	%	Value	%
U.S.A.	100	100.0	300	100.0	600	100.0	1,350	90.0
Total	100	100.0	300	100.0	600	100.0	1,500	100.0

Grand Total

	Value	%	Value	%	Value	%	Value	%
U.S.A.	16,200	52.2	17,700	62.5	36,700	71.4	47,350	67.6
W. Germany	1,050	3.4	1,400	4.9	1,700	3.3		
Brazil	900	2.9	1,400	4.9	3,500	6.8		
Canada	2,000	6.5	2,200	7.8	1,500	2.9		
Japan	6,900	22.3	2,700	9.6	2,200	4.3		
Other	3,950	12.7	2,900	10.3	5,800	11.3		
Total	31,000	100.0	28,300	100.0	51,400	100.0	70,000	100.0

Source: *Survey of Venezuelan Market*, Caracas, December 1980
*Estimates

(Lockheed, Systems Development Corporation, U.S. Department of Energy) and one Canadian. Thus for these telematic connections have been one way. This should change as soon as the Venezuelan data bank for the oil industry comes into being. An agreement with the U.S. Energy Department provides for two way use. Whatever the case, data on the Venezuelan oil industry is already circulated largely through the intermediary of technical cooperation agreements made by the former heads of the foreign companies that have now been nationalized. This availability of data is also due to the fact that the nationalized oil industry has given the processing of its information to consulting firms which use telematic networks situated outside Venezuela. Thus, since 1978, some of these consultants regularly use the resources of the Cybernet network (see Sutz, 1982).

The "unequal development of the state," according to a statement of a Venezuelan social scientist (see de la Cruz, 1981), gives rise to great discontinuity between the various agencies of the state itself. One can distinguish vanguard or advanced zones, rearguard or backward zones, and, finally, zones in transition, all of which have incorporated technological innovations, primarily computers, in varying degrees. This asynchronous technological modernization of the state is all the more striking when one considers that by 1979 the Venezuelan government was the largest client of the data processing industry. (See Table 3.1.)

> Now that the Government owns the oil industry, the major steel company, iron mining, alumina and aluminium producers, basic petrochemicals, shares in the 3 major airlines and the most prominent cargo shipping line, 5 of the largest banks, etc. it is not surprising that their share of total GNP is calculated to be in excess of 75%. (Final Report, 1980)

In the middle of 1981, Caracas, for the first time, used the SOI (System of Orientation and Information), the first teletext for public use in Latin America. Opting for the Canadian system, Telidon, the Venezuelan government has installed terminals in certain public places in the capital. There, one can find all the information one desires on administrative services. An extension of the system is envisaged for other regions of the country and there is a possibility of its being connected to Venezuelan households, where information, which in 1982 was available only at certain fixed places in Caracas could be obtained on television screens.

Disputes within the state

The case of Colombia shows that computers do not necessarily penetrate a society through the most advanced economic sectors, but their use may be propelled by other circles which play an active role in the social process. The place occupied by professional and technician groups in the creation of use values for technology indicates once more that the state is not an abstract and homogeneous entity, but the site where multiple interests and points of view enter into dispute. The construction of a national system of information in Colombia has led to numerous discussions which have highlighted the role of technicians and specialists.

The definition of the concept of information was the center of the debate, involving the different conceptions of the usefulness of information and the type of information to favor. For some, librarians and archivists, the value of information was in classification and reference; academics were considered by these specialists as having priority. For others, who intervened later in the debate and who contributed from their experience of technical assistance in official agencies in contact with industry and agriculture, information was an ingredient for research in, and the resolution of problems linked, to production.

The debate which had begun in 1969 and 1970 was taken up again in 1978, when other persons linked to planning organizations attempted to give a second wind to the National System of Information, which had functioned primarily as a system to aid in production and had never succeeded in completely reaching its objectives for want of technological and financial means.

This group of newcomers, primarily economists and computer specialists, were supported by the National Centre of Scientific Research (Colciencias), and demanded that a data bank be established which would provide systematically a historical record of employment, wages, and the behavior of the national economy. They proposed that the principal governmental units be equipped with video terminals, of which the first users would be those responsible for developing sector policies.

Several factors held up the project. Among these were the mobility of the public servants; the loss, by the public sector, of its most skilled professionals attracted by the advantages of the private sector (as in many other countries, the public sector in Colombia plays the role of a training ground); the crisis of the university system which was incapable of retaining its engineers, economists, and computer scientists and offered only mediocre conditions for careers in teaching and research. Another factor altered the course of the project: "The small number of Colombian specialists in this area explains the importance taken on by highly personalized projects which, because of this personalization, are highly vulnerable," noted the director of a research project in Bogota.

It is in this context that a new protagonist arose: the SER (Inter-Disciplinary Center of Independent Professionals), a private, nonprofit organization where professionals linked to the National System of Information worked. In the face of official shortcomings, the SER proposed to accommodate a data bank that would correspond to the one outlined by the former staff of the official planning body. This private institution offered certain advantages (above all in respect to the difficulties met by the administration): stability, efficiency, neutrality, and a big 370/145 computer offered by IBM! One question then dominated the debate. Could the state consign to a private institution, whatever its nature, data on the running of the country that some judged to be confidential?

In fact, however, the real question that no one openly poses lies elsewhere and is identical to the one created by the Panama project. How can one interpret the increasing role of an institution, admittedly private, but above all composed of researchers and engineers, both young and old, all trained in the school of cybernetics and "systems theory"? In a country with a long tradition of critical sociology, this sliding towards theoreticians in the management of the social system takes on a symbolic aspect.

3. Mexico: The State as Actor

The importance of the nationalized sector

Of all Latin American countries, Mexico has offered the most favorable environment for data processing activities. Numerous reasons explain the Mexican mode of computer institutionalization: the foreground role of the state in economic expansion, the strongly monopolist concentration of local enterprises, the notorious presence of transnational corporations, and a relatively widespread consumption of electronic appliances, stimulated, among other factors, by the intense contraband trade all along the frontier with the United States. The figures speak for themselves: the Mexican computer market underwent continual growth of the order of 30% a year between 1973 and 1977. In 1980, installations of equipment also increased 175% in comparison to 1979. By that year, Mexico had absorbed a quarter of the importations of data processing material destined for Latin America.

Since the installation of the first computers in 1956, the Mexican state has played a vanguard role in the promotion of computer technology. The legal framework that governs the state institutions permits an official presence in many aspects of socioeconomic life. The rapid expansion of the para-state sector has gone hand in hand with a growing use of computer resources. Thus, between 1970 and 1976, so-called "decentralized bodies" increased threefold, from 45 to 128. Enterprises in which the state had major participation increased from 39 to 524. In 1975, more than half of the total investments of the country were in public enterprises. The extent of Mexico's oil resources has only accelerated these investments (Mexico Secretaria, 1981).

But the productive sector linked to the state is not the only one to have incorporated computers in its activities. The computer has also been a favored tool for the modernization of public services. Health and education, which are among the services affecting the largest number of people, are increasingly relying on computers in their administration.

The relation between users and the state is thus increasingly mediated. Very recently, the computer and no longer the teacher has decided in which school primary pupils will continue their studies. The computer not only allows for greater flexibility in the functions that come under the jurisdiction of the state, but provides a guarantee of exactness and impartiality. The new electoral roll drawn up in Mexico, where all citizens having the right to vote are listed for the first time, was prepared on automatic systems. The vast promotional campaign launched for this event enhanced the role of the computer: frauds and electoral manipulations were no longer to be feared, from the moment the "machine" recorded, classified, and delivered a voter's card to everyone.

The movement towards monopolist concentration in industrial, commercial, and financial sectors, has found an efficient instrument of consolidation in computers. Stresses an official study:

> The telecomputers which have facilitated communication between banking consortiums has increased the power of the leading groups. Carrying out more and more operations, opening offices and branches all over the country, and even overseas, these financial groups exercise strong pressure as demanders of hardware and of teleprocessing systems necessary for sending an increasing volume of information on their transactions rapidly in all directions. (Mexico Secretaria, 1981)[2]

With the nationalization of banks decreed in September 1982, the Mexican state is more than even in control of computers.

According to the journal *Datamation,* half of the personal computers in Mexico are smuggled in. Although it is difficult in these conditions to advance a reliable figure on the total stock of microcomputers in use in the country, it is estimated that there are about 20,000 units. The social use of these computers generally differs from that in the U.S.

---

[2] In order to clearly understand this process of concentration, it should be mentioned that, before nationalization, the two biggest banks in Mexico (Bancomer and Banamex) held 54% of the total of the national banking system and were situated in the 86th and 88th ranks respectively in the world classification of *Fortune.* This made Mexican banking activity one of the strongest monopoly structures in the world (likewise for its television system!). Unlike other Latin American countries, the Mexican banking system includes only one foreign establishment—Citibank. With 25 million savings accounts and 4 million checking accounts, Mexican private banks maintain over 40 agencies abroad. Furthermore, directly integrated in the economic tissue of the country, the banker and the industrialist were one and the same. (For a critical vision of the nationalization of the banks, see Castaneda (1982).

In Mexico, as in most other developing countries, there is no dp hobby trade. As a result, personal computers have been primarily selling in the small business market. Most small system buyers are first-time computer users who are using the new gear to replace old electromechanical accounting devices. (Gardner, 1981)

Insistent questions

During the last decade and particularly since 1977, when the first official organ responsible for computer policy in Mexico was created, the theme has assumed a growing importance. It is symptomatic that the President for the 1982–1988 term, Miguel de la Madrid, comes from the Secretariat of programming and budgeting, a relatively new body which, among other responsibilities, concentrates on data processing activities and decides on guidelines for the development of the computer sector. Certain questions crop up unceasingly in conversations, debates, and speeches on the theme. Among the changes that have intervened in the national socioeconomic system, which ones have most favored the model of adoption and dissemination of computer technology implanted in Mexico? In which areas can the most flagrant discontinuities be found between the model of computer development followed until now and the model of historical evolution of the country? To what extent are current and potential users submitted to the oligopolistic control instituted on the market by the big transnational corporations which dominate the technological and commercial development of this sector? What are the risks for the country of seeing the deterioration of its capacity for regulating changes in the sociopolitical system, if control over national computer development is lost? What real options are there for national industry, teaching, and research institutions, and for the state apparatus itself, on the manufacture of hardware, training, the use of human resources, and development of software, which would enable Mexico to fill, or at least diminish, the gap between its national computer development and those of other countries (Mexico Secretaria, 1981)? [3]

In 1981, especially at the beginning of the Presidential campaign,

---

[3] In May 1982, Mexico laid the first foundations of its industrial computer policy of which the goal is to construct a local industry through import substitutions. Over 45 companies have already solicited the authorization to manufacture computers or related hardware. Within the terms of the law, firms can be 100% owners of their subsidiaries, but must use a high proportion of Mexican components.

the antinomy between politics/technocracy reflected the underlying pre-occupations of Mexican society. Is technology simply an instrument for attaining collective objectives defined by politics, or a way of justifying projects which only find their legitimacy in technocratic efficiency and modernity? On the response to this question, which sums up the earlier formulations, depends the coming future of Mexico.

If, unlike in the United States, the microcomputer has not found any outlets in the leisure domain, electronic games have won over adults who buy them for their children. They have also won over the children, conditioned by a cultural and advertising environment that promotes this type of pastime. In Mexico, as in most countries (industrialized or not), the game or toy is the first step for an individual to enter the world of computers, thus contributing towards "naturalizing" one's relation with advanced technologies. Three of the most important transnational toy firms are installed in Mexico: Lili Lady, a subsidiary of General Mills since 1960; CIPSA, linked to the American firm, Mattel; and Plastimarx, a subsidiary of Fisher-Price, a division of the agro-food conglomerate, Quaker Oats. These firms, pioneers in electronic toy production, controlled 60% of the Mexican market by the end of the 1970s.

In 1976, 80% of the toys sold in Mexico came from free trade zones. Mattel was one of the first firms to set up in the town of Mexicali, situated in the subcontracting zone in the North of the country (see NACLA, 1975, p. 17).[4] True to form, the free zone is a center for contraband goods destined for the interior. Official reports are unanimous in denouncing this fact.

---

[4] On the toy industry in Mexico, see the reports of the Centre Français du Commerce Exterieur (CFCE), Paris.

4. Chile: The Masked State

Economic policy: a superpolicy

"From both the public and private points of view, one must take account of the fact that there exists in this country a superpolicy: economic policy. This is what dictates a principle of liberty, linked to the decisions of private firms and, in its own way, public firms. This is why a more specific and precise policy towards computers has not developed at a government level," affirmed a Chilean specialist in a personal interview.

In September 1981, Chile inaugurated one of the first public tele-processing networks in Latin America. This system allows firms and institutions to have access to all available computer resources. Chile is thus attempting to obtain an optimal use of its hardware capacity and generalize access to specialized information, computers, and data bank systems, not only in Chile but especially in other countries.

In its initial stage, the public network of data transmission links the towns of Santiago, Valparaiso, and Concepción. The project provides for the progressive integration of all the towns in the country into the system. These three large computer centers are connected to the American Telenet network.

The economic policy imposed in Chile means that the expansion of computers follows the ups and downs of the market, as registered by the business demand. The philosophy of this policy, inspired by the precepts of Milton Friedman, makes the criteria of profitability and efficiency the central pivot around which all institutions orbit. ECOM (Empresa Nacional de Computación e Información Ltda), on which the public tele-processing network depends, was created in 1968 as a state organ. Under the influence of the economic policy of the government established after the military coup of 1973, it has become an autarchical enterprise, which has to finance itself by selling its services on the market, where it competes with private firms even where state markets are concerned. Thus, in 1981, two public departments abandoned ECOM (which still conserves its semi-official status in spite of everything) and gave their data processing to other private firms.

The growth of the stock of computers in Chile began in 1975 when the government temporarily reduced import taxes for computer products for the first time. In one year, IBM introduced more hardware in Chile than during the preceding 13 years. Soon afterwards, the scale of import taxes was definitively fixed (foreign computer products are only taxed 10%). By opening its frontiers in this sector as well as in others, Chile has renounced the protection of possible future national computer industry. "In our conditions, given in particular the limited size of our market, we must aspire to become like Hong Kong," declared the Chilean computer scientist quoted above.

The logic of the market

According to this same source, the logic of the market, which proves to be the organizing axis of society, commands not only the process of development, but also the attitudes adopted in the face of international legislation which tends to regulate transborder information flows as well as attitudes towards privacy. "If one is consistent with the criteria of free imports and exports, there is no reason why information should be treated differently," affirms the specialist quoted above.

Obviously, in this reasoning, any regulation would lead to an alteration of this liberty, an open market having nothing to hide. He continues:

> There is no risk of computers being used in Chile to limit individual liberties. Policies based on the market tend to reduce the interference of the state in everyday life. Authority is not used to limit the action of the individual but to lay down the rules of the game. The government simply says to the citizen: here are the possible choices. But it does not point out which one the citizen must choose. If things are tackled in a pragmatic instead of an ideological fashion, there is no contradiction in practice between the liberty of the market, which implies the non-control of individual actions, and an authoritarian government. Where our case is curious is that authoritarianism is at the service of a complete change of what was usual beforehand, i.e., the presence of the state in all affairs. In Chile, the authoritarian state paradoxically uses its authority to reduce its authority over individuals. Thus, it is pointless thinking that information can affect privacy. This could be true in European countries where the state interferes strongly in the life of every citizen. In Sweden or France for example; the systems of dependence imposed by the state through collective mechanisms like Social Security, pensions, etc., increase the risk of state domination over individuals. It would be very difficult to go back-

wards. The benefits of the present system are felt in numerous sectors. In the last few years, for example, we have bought more television sets, radios, and cars than in the whole preceding history of Chile. When people see the benefits of free choice, with the increase of prosperity, they will become more conservative and become the best defenders of the system. No, I don't think Orwell's *1984* is possible here.

Information *is* national security

The axioms of free choice offered by the market are the basis of several discourses—sometimes contradictory—which legitimize the Chilean regime. To the vision of a state, removed from everyday life, but which imposes the ground rules, i.e., the essential norms on which society is erected, is opposed another which claims for the state the decisive role of sovereign arbiter over the life of individuals and institutions.

General José Mutis, president of ECOM feels that, "the state should be equipped at the highest level with an organ responsible for orienting computer development, especially in the public sector." He enumerated several projects that could be launched: to improve judicial administration in order to reduce the slowness of searches in jurisprudence and information; to unify the different files (fiscal, electoral, realty) into a single system, allowing for an immediate and rigorously exact identification of people (*La Tercera de la Hora*, 1981).

For more than a century, responsibility for the register of births, marriages, and deaths in Santiago de Chile has been given to a person bearing the title of Advocate-Director of the Civil Register. In 1980, the emphasis previously put on the judicial side (one had to be a lawyer) was shifted to the administrative. The responsibility for this service was entrusted to a civil engineer who specialized in computer science. The project of the new director consists in recording all the legal information available on each citizen on a single file, including identification data, criminal records, and one's civil history and transport offenses.

This reorganization of the civil register, planned in three stages, is producing, in the Director's own words, "an integral, draconian change and will give birth to an absolutely new system, the gradual introduction of a new technology being unadvisable." Once the rationalization of the central service is carried out, the second stage will consist in connecting the 12 regions of the country to the computer of the central office of identification through terminals. In computing circles, this project of a big data bank of information on citizens is regarded as perfectly realizable. It is emphasized that it will be useful for everything touched on the relation between the citizen and the state (S. Prenafeta, 1980).

In the conception of the President of ECOM, the relation that ought to exist between the state and information is one in which the latter is necessarily directive. In order to make himself understood, he borrows a military metaphor:

> What does a strategy of information need? The concept of the assessment of a situation used by the staff of the armed forces rests on information. . . . This concept of assessment of the situation, in a neighboring methodology, is today called "decision making technique." It is a mathematical concept which consists in introducing variables in a decision matrix, for which the calculation is made by computer. But the process of decision followed by a troop commander for a tactical operation or strategy and that of a managing director when he decides to buy, sell, expand, or carry out such and such a project, both require basically the same thing: the greatest possible quantity of information and elements with which to make a choice. (*La Tercera de la Hora,* 1981)

The doctrine of national security, which seems to evaporate with time but which continues to be the last resort for legitimization of the authoritarian state, has different faces. It imposes, on the one hand, the organic framework of social control, apparently diluted in free competition, and demands, on the other, a strategic role in the constitution of another institutionality, founded on a new schema of social relations. The notorious development of social coercion, the reinforcement of security mechanisms and state authority, thanks to the injection of modern technology which tends to suppress manifestations of a stifled civil society, is proving to be necessary up until the day where a new conformity succeeds in imposing a new consensus.

"Whoever possesses information, also possesses power," declared the same President of ECOM. Information and its technology are looked on as basic tools for the restoration of order in the whole of society. "Information *is* national security," he stressed.

5. Brazil: The Integrating State

The history of telecommunications

The development of computer policy in Brazil has its roots in the history of its telecommunications and, if one wishes to go further, in the overall model of society which began to take shape just before 1964. The study of the institutionalization of computers in this country allows us to grasp, better than anywhere else in Latin America, the link existing between information production and distribution systems and the totality of the social process.

As often happens, this history has been affected by diverse contradictions, notably within the armed forces, which imposed their conception of change in the 1960s. There were also contradictions between the military officers and the civilians who participated in this change: contradictions between the diverse branches of institutions which worked toward the constitution of a national system of communication and information; contradictions between groups linked to transnationals and those animated by a wish for national autonomy in the industrial domain: contradictions, finally, within the professional and technical layers which were formed through the expansion of the information industry. This set of oppositions is played out within an ideological space where two powerful poles of attraction intervene: national identity and national security. These poles sometimes converge and merge into one another to the point that it becomes difficult to distinguish them.

The major characteristic of Brazilian telecommunications towards 1962 was dispersed and insufficient networks. (See *Revista Nacional de Telecommunicações,* 1980a.) The Brazilian telephone company, a subsidiary of the Canadian group, Brazilian Traction, had more than 60% of the country's telephones under its control; it occupied by far the first position among the several thousand franchise holders authorized to exploit this technology. The vagueness of the definition of responsibilities of federal, state, and municipal authorities granting of concessions contributed to making planning difficult at a national level as well as the imposing of norms and administrative and technical rules for telecommunications services. Added to this was the reluctance of private investors resulting from controls established over subscription tariffs. Brazil had barely two telephone lines for 100 inhabitants, an extremely low rate. Connections were often nonexistent between large-sized cities and sometimes even between the capital and cities in the interior.

The system of radio broadcasting had no unified regulation. There was no register listing all the radio transmitters in the country. In the absence of a microwave network for television retransmissions, most transmitters had only a local or, at best, regional range.

Finally, postal services were running largely at a loss, were unreliable and did not cover the whole territory.

In 1962, the "Brazilian code of telecommunications" was promulgated, which gave to the state the responsibility of installing and exploiting telecommunications networks as well as confirming the private status of radio broadcasting. Two years before taking power in the coup that overthrew President Joao Goulart, the staff command of the armed forces (particularly the navy and army) had applied pressure to have this code take effect as quickly as possible. The strategic role of telecommunications, which was to allow it to "integrate" the dislocated whole of the country, had not escaped them.

In 1965, EMBRATEL, the Brazilian telephone firm, was created. Its motto was: "Communication is integration." The following year, the government decided to acquire all of the shares of the company, which until then had been owned by the Canadian firm. EMBRATEL was given very precise tasks: to install a microwave network between the federated states; to set up and exploit the terrestrial satellite station (which was to be inaugurated in 1969); and to facilitate the construction of a national television network. The Ministry of Telecommunications was instituted in 1967, public works and transports from then on coming under other ministries. The private system Rede Globo appeared in 1965 and television transmission on a national scale in 1970. The expansion of the telephone was slower (from 1.3 million in 1962 to 2 million in 1970).

The creation of TELEBRAS in 1972 marked the culminating point of efforts to unify the system. TELEBRAS brought together firms created in each state, whose role was to integrate the system and assure its planning locally. In 1976, TELEBRAS founded a center specializing in the research and development of communications systems. This center, installed at Campinas, pursues the fundamental objective of reducing the country's dependence in this area. The results were not long in coming. Five years after its creation, the center at Campinas, perfected an optical fiber communication technology which placed Brazil among the vanguard countries in this activity.

The end of the public monopoly?

In 1981, TELEBRAS entered the world of telematics with the installation in Sao Paulo, with the participation of the French firm Matra, of an experimental videotex system, destined for large firms and about a thousand households. Information providers of the network include the principal commercial firms and media of the city and state of Sao Paulo.

This breakthrough into telematics has not been without its tensions. On the one hand, the directors of TELEBRAS are seeking to conserve the monopoly of innovation in these new communication sectors. On the other, certain financial circles, seeking to reduce the functions of TELE-BRAS, are doing everything to ensure that these networks are put under the control of the private sector. The priority is no longer on the telephone itself. "In the future, telephony will be a service derived from telematic networks," declared a director of TELEBRAS, pointing out the key to the future.

The discussions over the development of a new code, which would replace that of 1962 and legislate both on telecommunications and audiovisual media, have not only brought out the conflicts of interest existing between the private and public sectors.

The declarations of the Minister of Communications in September 1980 indicated an unexpected complexity.

> My personal inclination is for the private sector. The public sector has admittedly given good results up until now. But will state-owned enterprises be flexible and dynamic enough to react to new challenges? I don't think the government has to directly assure the exploitation of services. It will always obviously have to control, supervise and fix the norms . . . Here, I am opening up a debate. Given the level of development attained by Brazilian telecommunications, I really wonder if we should continue to apply the solution adopted several years ago to this sector. My opinion on this subject has been influenced by conversations with General Eduardo Corrado, of the Argentine Secretariat of Telecommunications. Argentina is in the process of opening up this sector to private capital . . . When I see a man as lucid as General Corrado envisage the problem in this way, I ask myself: how long will we defend at all costs the thesis of state control? (*Revista Nacional de Telecommunicações*, 1980b)

The matrix of an industrial strategy

Unlike the rest of Latin America, the advent of computers in Brazil has been accompanied by an effort at industrial development in this sector, supported by the state.[5] These attempts at a computer policy are in line with the general principles established by the military government after the 1964 coup. These principles are based on a doctrine of national security and a desire for national sovereignty.

It is in this context that the need to create Brazilian technology which can guarantee the independence of this sector emerges, along with a need to assure the supply of such equipment for the armed forces. The Federal Data Processing Service (SERPRO), began to operate in 1965, at the same time as the first computers in the Ministry of Finance. SERPRO, created with the objective of "modernizing the fiscal apparatus," very quickly received orders from other administrative agencies. After setting up a research and development center, and on the basis of experience acquired in software manufacture, SERPRO is attempting to move into hardware manufacture. The production of the first equipment, destined for its own needs and for clients in the public sector, began in 1969. This production policy was expected to profit from two factors: the protection of the domestic market and the possibility of negotiating with certain transnational suppliers. (Figure 3.2 depicts Bra-

---

[5] Other attempts to construct national computer industries have certainly taken place in other Latin American countries, but, in general, they have not succeeded in emerging into active policies motivated by consistent backing. In Argentina, for example, research undertaken in the 1970s led to the beginnings of production. In Mexico, certain higher education establishments, e.g., the National Autonomous University or the National Polytechnic Institute, made progress in the perfection of hardware and software. However, Cuba, along with Brazil, is the country that has made the greatest effort to establish a basic policy with the intent of establishing a national industry. The National Institute of Automatized Systems and Computer Technology (INSAC), founded in 1976, is clear evidence of the desire to develop the necessary technology. As early as 1970, a group of researchers at the University of Havana, proposed the construction of a digital computer to resolve the problems of rail transport of sugar cane. They perfected a prototype of the CID 201 minicomputer, the first such device to have been entirely conceived and constructed by Cuban specialists. Since then Cuba has continued to establish itself, within the common market of socialist countries (CAME), as a country specializing in the production of computers adapted to specific needs (minicomputer CID 300-10, CID-02, and alphanumeric video-terminals among others). The sugar industry has a national data transmission network available that has been made possible through Cuba's national technology. Other projects are being developed, for example, the creation of specialized networks for various industries and for the banking system. Also important is the policy of introducing the computer into teaching and the practical computer training program which are present at all levels of the curriculum. On this subject, see the document presented by the Cuban delegation (1980); See also the paper by E. Gonzalez-Manet (1981).

FIGURE 3.2 BRAZIL'S INDUSTRIAL INFORMATICS STRATEGY

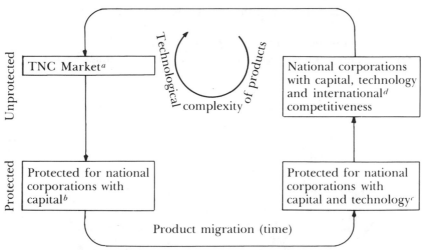

Source: SEI, Brasilia, Brazil, 1982

[a]Not protected (transnational corporations are welcome, they export and use state-of-the-art technology), because national corporations are not yet able to enter production.

[b]Protected for national corporations (which can use foreign technologies) because they are able to invest, but do not yet have their own technology.

[c]Protected for those national corporations that have their own capital and technology, but are not yet fully competitive on the international market.

[d]Protected barriers are lowered because national corporations are competitive on the international market. Local technology is still required and safe guards are taken to maintain the control of the national industry.

zils industrial informatics strategy.) In 1968, SERPRO, profiting from the appearance of the microcomputer, decided to abandon the old IBM system using punched cards, in order to adopt Olivetti microcomputers. Based on a prototype from the American company, Hewlett-Packard, technicians from SERPRO developed a nationally produced model of peripheral hardware. In 1977 it manufactured more than 2000 entry terminals, better adapted to its needs than imported ones.

The Brazilian aeronautics industry followed the same path. The Brazilian aeronautics firm, EMBRAER, under the direction of the Ministry of Aeronautics, started an import substitution policy for armaments in 1970. The existence of an internal market made possible the production of both military and commercial ("bandeirantes") airplanes. The competition between transnational firms and an understanding of their relative vulnerability makes possible the acquisition of foreign technology for the construction of a country's own technology. The American company CESSNA having refused a technology transfer, EMBRAER signed an agreement with another American company, Piper

Aircraft which authorized it to modify the design of the aircraft in order to adapt it to its own standards.[6]

The telecommunications field did not follow the same path, and the industry generally remained under the dominance of transnational firms. By putting the emphasis on distribution rather than on production, Brazil failed to benefit from the advantages its policy of reserving the domestic market had brought in other sectors. In 1980, several measures were taken, including the nationalization of a part of the foreign capital. Some professional circles, relying on the technological change to digital equipment, felt that the moment had come to make a substantial change in the existing situation. A Brazilian telecommunications engineer had no hesitation in describing the change as a "multinational cartel regulated by the government." But the official decision was diferred, with the consequences we have noted (see chapter 2).

The construction of a nationally produced microcomputer

The first government project for computer construction got off the ground in 1971. A "Special Work Group" (GTE), under the authority of the Ministry of Marine and backed by the Ministry of Planning, was given this task. Its objective was to "plan, develop, and construct a prototype computer for naval operations." Several Brazilian universities previously had carried out projects for intelligent terminals. The Institute of Physics of the University of Sao Paulo had even succeeded in building a computer. One of the explicit objectives of the GTE was to bring together a work team from the several universities.

In 1972, the Commission of Coordination for Electronic Processing (CAPRE) was created under the auspices of the Ministry of Planning. Its goal was to establish a computer policy and to control imports and national firms wishing to form alliances with foreign firms. It was on the initiative of CAPRE that measures were taken in 1977 for the protection of the microcomputer market, to be henceforth reserved for national firms. The firm COBRA (Computadoras e Sistemas Brasileiros) started operations in 1974. In 1981, it was the largest computer factory belonging to the state. The creation of this factory was a result of the work of the GTE. Some of the technicians of SERPRO transferred to this new firm, whose task was to "develop, produce, and commercialize computers in the country." In 1977, five national firms were selected to operate in the field of micro- and minicomputers. They were assured in advance of a protected domestic market. With the acquisition of foreign tech-

---

[6] On the history of the Brazilian war industry, see Brigagão (1981).

TABLE 3.2. AUTHORIZED BRAZILIAN MANUFACTURERS

Company	Model	Technology	Description
COBRA—Computadores e Sistemas Brasileiros S.A.	COBRA-300	COBRA	Up to 48KB cpu Small single-user micro Based on floppy disks
	COBRA-400	SYCOR (U.S.)	Up to 64KB cpu mini-computer with a model oriented to data entry and MUMPS
	COBRA-530	COBRA	Up to 512KB cpu with future expansion to 1 MB
EDISA—Eletronica Digital S.A.	ED-300	FUJITSU (Japan)	Up to 64KB cpu Similar to IBM System 3
LABO Eletronica S.A.	LABO 8034	NIXDORF (W. Germany)	Up to 256KB cpu Similar to Nixdorf 8870–1
SID—Sistemas de Informaçao Distribuida S.A.	SID-500	LOGABAX (France)	Up to 64KB cpu Similar to DEC PDP-11/34
SISCO—Sistemas e Computadores S.A.	SCC-5000	SISCO	Up to 64KB cpu Similar to DEC PDP-8
	MB-800	SISCO	Up to 256KB cpu Similar to DG NOVA 3

Source: "Betting on Brazil," by Marc Burbridge, *Datamation,* May 1981.

nology, these firms should be able to generate national models in five years. Here also, Brazil profited from the possibility of negotiating with small foreign firms. In spite of the pressure by Data General on the American government for an embargo on this technology transfer, the firm Sycor was one of the smaller firms that sold its know-how in computerization of banking transactions to COBRA. In 1981, the national industry had succeeded in capturing 14% of the Brazilian market (in value) and 42% (in volume), COBRA having the lion's share, with 60%. 30% of the hardware sold by COBRA was bought by the financial sector (public and private banks), 28% by the service sector, 22% by industry and commerce, 18% by the government, and 1% by education (AEC, 1981).[7] (See Tables 3.2, 3.3, and 3.4 for statistics of Brazilian computer manufactures, suppliers, and Brazilian built DP equipment.)

In October 1981, within the framework of the new privatization

---

[7] AEC also publishes a journal, *Lingua de Cobra.* See in particular the August–September 1980 issue.

TABLE 3.3. MAJOR BRAZILIAN DP SUPPLIERS

1980 Ranking by Revenue	Company	Estimate DP Revenues (in $millions)		Capital Registered in Brazil (in $millions)	Number of Employees
		1979	1980		
1	IBM	350	330	130	5
2	COBRA*	70	104	9	2
3	BURROUGHS	100**	100**	2**	2**
4	SID*	19	30	5	.8
5	LABO*	5	22	2	.4
6	EDISA*	7	13	3	.3
7	SISCO*	.6	10	3	.3
8	GLOBUS*	.8	10	.8	1
9	ELEBRA INFORMATICA*	.5	9	2	.1
10	SCOPUS*	5	9	.8	.4
11	HONEY-BULL	7	8	3**	.1**
12	POLYMAX*	.4	7	.4	.2
13	MICROLAB*	2	6	1	.3
14	COENCISA*	5	5	2	.2
15	PROLOGICA*	.2	5	.05	.2

Source: Ibid.
*Data on these companies furnished by DIGIBRAS, a federal-owned company that provides technical and financial support to national hardware manufacturers.
**Company-furnished data.

TABLE 3.4 BRAZILIAN BUILT DP EQUIPMENT

TYPE OF PRODUCT

COMPANY	MEDIUM & LARGE COMPUTERS	MINI & MIDI COMPUTERS	MICROCOMPUTERS	PERSONAL COMPUTERS	PROCESS CONTROL	ELECTRONIC ACCOUNTING	DATA ENTRY	WORD PROCESSING	INTELLIGENT TERMINALS	TERMINALS	BANK TERMINALS	SALES TERMINALS	SERIAL PRINTERS	LINE PRINTERS	MAGNETIC DISK	FLOPPY DISK	MAGNETIC TAPE	KEYBOARDS	MODEMS	TAPE CARTRIDGE	REMOTE MONITORING	PROGRAMMABLE CONTROLS
BURROUGHS	▲					●								●	●							
COBRA		●	●		●		●		●	●	●				●							
COENCISA																				●		
CONPART																●						
DIGILAB													●									
DIGIPONTO																			●			
DIGIREDE							●															

TABLE 3.4 (*Continued*)

TYPE OF PRODUCT

COMPANY	MEDIUM & LARGE COMPUTERS	MINI & MIDI COMPUTERS	MICROCOMPUTERS	PERSONAL COMPUTERS	PROCESS CONTROL	ELECTRONIC ACCOUNTING	DATA ENTRY	WORD PROCESSING	INTELLIGENT TERMINALS	TERMINALS	BANK TERMINALS	SALES TERMINALS	SERIAL PRINTERS	LINE PRINTERS	MAGNETIC DISK	FLOPPY DISK	MAGNETIC TAPE	KEYBOARDS	MODEMS	TAPE CARTRIDGE	REMOTE MONITORING	PROGRAMMABLE CONTROLS
DISMAC				▲		●																
EDISA		●				●																
ELEBRA ELECTRONICA																			●	▲		
ELEBRA INFORMATICA													●		●	●						
EMBRACOMP							●		●													
EXATA							●															
FLEXIDISK																●						
GLENDATA							●															
GLOBUS													●	●			●					
HEWLETT-PACKARD				▲																		
IBM	●								●				●				▲					
ITAU										●												
KUHN																			●			
LABO		●				●																
MDA								●														
MICROLAB															●		●				●	
MULTIDIGIT															●							
OLIVETTI						●	●															
OZ-ELETRONICA																				●		
PARKS									●											●		
POLYMAX			●					●														
PROLOGICA							●															
PULSA																						●
QUARTZIL			●				●															
RACIMEC										●												
SCOPUS									●	●												
SID		●	●			●	●		●	●												
SISCO		●	●	●		●	●		●	●												
TECLA										●												
TECNODATA											●											
ZANTHUS										●												

Source: Ibid.
● Manufactured in 1980   ▲ Manufactured in 1981

policy encouraged by the government, COBRA was among the first enterprises to be offered to the private sector. One year before, the government had authorized IBM and Burroughs to manufacture medium-sized computers in Brazil. This decision provoked a hue and cry from numerous professional sectors linked to computers and from the staff of COBRA. "In contempt of the efforts of Brazilian technicians and managers and as usual by a unilateral and irrevocable decision, the Special Secretariat for Informatics, has dealt a severe blow to the protected market policy which was the rule in this sector. This policy constitutes one of the essential elements of a feasible model of technological independence in the computer field" (*Tribuna da Imprensa*, Rio de Janeiro, August 8, 1980, p. 10).

Between democracy and strong state

The Brazilian Special Secretariat for Informatics, SEI, was established in 1979. The right arm of the Brazilian government, the SEI established a project of overall use of computers for the development of the country and has been given the responsibility of carrying it out. "Society must prepare itself for the post-industrial era," affirmed an SEI public servant, thus indicating the strategic importance of data processing.

In a document that serves as a permanent point of reference for the staff, the director of this secretariat gave free rein to his enthusiasm for the expected computerized society in Brazil.

> The technical difficulties which have up until now prevented the majority of citizens from participating in political decisions are in the process of being resolved owing to the revolution in computer and communications technology. It must be appreciated that in a computerized society, a referendum will be as simple to carry out as an opinion poll is today, with the single exception that a referendum will be quicker and cost infinitely less . . . We are on the threshold of a golden age of humanity where decisions will be made by consensus. It will no longer be a question of repeating old slogans and worn-out watchwords to carry out referendums of which the bases are known in advance. Having access to all the information on what is at stake, citizens, whose participation will count for something, will choose in a sovereign and conscious manner. (Gennari Netto, 1981)

The SEI depends on the National Security Council. It is significant that this Secretariat is established and that its objectives are fixed within the framework of the principle of national security at the very moment when the theme of the computerization of society is beginning to assume a primordial interest for a new national political model. "Computers are a strategic domain for this country," pointed out a young director of

SEI, fresh from a two year training course with French firms Thomson and Matra. "Experience has shown the importance of the existence of a strong state for the expansion of these strategic areas," he continued. The creation of this Secretariat under the auspices of the military authorities appeared to be somewhat incompatible with the desire to enlarge the rights of civil society that the political overtures initiated at the end of 1978 seemed to promise.[8]

Towards a "Silicon Valley" in Sao Paulo?

The last chapter of the on-going history of Brazilian computer policy, opened with the intervention of the SEI representative at the IIIrd Brazilian Colloquium on microelectronics, held at the University of Campinas in June 1981. The government announced its intention of creating a technological-industrial complex in Campinas devoted to the national development of microelectronics. Three important centers of research on electronic components and semiconductors, linked to Telebras and the University, are already functioning there. This complex, which makes operative the alliance between industry, the university, and state agencies, will manufacture integrated circuits, by using, primarily, the results of university research. The Campinas project brings to mind, making due allowances for size, the so-called "Silicon Valley" in California, where researchers from the University of California Berkeley and Stanford University and the two hundred largest electronic firms in the United States work together.

The two Brazilian groups chosen for the construction of the first two factories of the complex are not lacking in experience, both in microprocessor production and in the use of computers in their firms. The banking group, ITAU, is specialized in the production of electronic hardware destined for banks and financial institutions. The group, Docas de Santos, has an electronics division, and, at the end of 1981, was on the list of possible buyers of COBRA.

This last stage enables us to measure the progress made under Brazilian computer policy and to appreciate the points of continuity and discontinuity since its beginnings. The state is now no longer necessarily the promoter or head of the firm, seeking to participate actively in the business market; but seems to prefer handing responsibility over to the

---

[8] A bill passed by the Brazilian Congress in October 1984 extends the ban on computer imports for eight years and widens the embargo to include all items containing microchips. The law will be enforced by a civilian group (18 members representing industry as well as government).

private sector. According to certain Brazilian researchers and technicians, the consequences of this delegation of power will not be limited to the economy. The example of the journal, *Dados e Idéias*, is a good example of this new policy. Published by SERPRO, this journal outlined its goals in its first issue in 1975: "Some programmers and analysts never question their work . . . up until the day when they are themselves questioned about the goals of the computer, its philosophy, and the problems it poses. Then, faced with these embarrassing questions, they will remember that there exists a journal which is interested in everything concerning data processing . . . ; a journal which attempts to discuss and analyze the technical, economic, political, and philosophical questions which are hidden behind the computer." Four years later, in 1979, *Dados* was taken over by a commercial publishing house. Nothing distinguishes it today from the other technical journals on the market. Several computer scientists from SERPRO who began critical discussions on their profession in *Dados e Idéias* have now moved on to other activities in the state.

The development of computers and microelectronics has created an increasingly large supply of researchers and technicians in Brazil. Some of them pose extremely pertinent questions on the uses and the social significance of the new technologies in their hands. Their practice is intimately linked to the desire to play an integral part in the production of an autonomous technology which is, moreover, the only guarantee of their own survival as professionals. "If the means of production do not use Brazilian technology, thousands of us, engineers, professionals, and scientists, will be cloistered in firms, the state apparatus, and universities. But we shall have no technological autonomy. We shall be confined to administrative work, outside our speciality, in firms, becoming bureaucrats in government organizations or sclerosed by university routine" (da Costa Marques, 1975–76).

6. The Role of Technicians

The lack of studies: a significant fact

Little work has been done in Latin America on the incorporation of the intellectual and professional groups into the technocratic structures of decision-making. Nor has the active participation of some representatives of these circles in the critique of existing social forms been sufficiently analyzed. Questioning the why and wherefore of this deficiency, especially on a continent where intellectuals have always played an important role in the historical process, would undoubtedly enable the criteria that have inspired the choice of tactics and political strategies to become known. It would then be possible to pinpoint the limits of certain theories on the functioning of society which perceive the professional strata only as tactical instruments for capturing the favor of the often undefined "middle classes." This would also enable us to discover the reasons why the forces of change have neglected the study of the status of science and technology in social relations.

We know that the incorporation of certain social groups into the projects of remodelling the state institutions and reorganizing the business sector is giving rise to strategic disputes. The Trilateral Commission, to which we owe the most pertinent diagnosis of the contemporary world crisis from the point of view of the capitalist powers and which has recommended draconian readjustments for the survival of the system, has made clear the extent to which the intellectual strata represent a new, key stake. A report published by the Trilateral Commission recognizes that a large number of intellectuals have chosen to criticize the established order and have contributed to the loss of legitimacy of old forms of social control, "their behavior contrasting with that of the also increasing numbers of technocratic and policy-oriented intellectuals." Noting the acuteness of the present conflict, the report continued:

> In an age of widespread secondary school and university education, the pervasiveness of the mass media, and the displacement of manual

labor by clerical and professional employees, this development constitutes a challenge to democratic government which is, potentially at least, as serious as those posed in the past by the aristocratic cliques, fascist movements, and communist parties. (Crozier, Huntington, and Watanuki, 1975, pp. 6–7)

"If the state is strong, it crushes us; if it is weak, we perish"

In their practice, some elements of the professional and technician strata of Latin America have assumed attitudes severely critical of the technocratic tendency inherent in the dynamic of power. The process of the institutionalization of computers, for example, had led some groups of technicians to question themselves on the autonomy of their knowledge and even the meaning of their work. This line of thinking has encouraged them to share their experience with other social strata, so as to associate them with the defining of policy for this sector. During its Second Congress in 1981, the Brazilian Association of Professional Data Processors had no hesitation in demanding that its members, "as citizens, widen the debate on the national computer policy to the whole of civil society and construct an alliance, based on common objectives, with the organizations of the working class" (Brazilian Association of Professional Data Processors, 1981; see also Millan and Hermes de Araujo, 1979).[9]

It would, however, be rash to pretend that the group espousing the refusal of technocracy, which includes some Latin American engineers and computer scientists, expresses the position of the majority. The worldwide tendency for the transfer of decisions of sector-based policies into the hands of technocrats has repercussions throughout the conti-

---

[9] Within the framework of an alliance between technicians and the different components of the popular movement, one must mention the initiative of IBASE (Instituto Brasileiro de analisis sociais e economicas) of Rio de Janeiro. A group of social science researchers, aided by computer engineers, have tried with a mini computer to "systematize and distribute basic information on the Brazilian and international situation. This information is addressed in particular to popular movements and organizations, such as unions, professional associations, and community groups. It is also addressed to institutions like universities, parties, and churches, linked to social movements and engaged in the transformation of society." Pursuing the "democratization of information," IBASE proposes to, "gather the socioeconomic information produced by already existing organs and popular movements. We propose to integrate, aggregate, and transform this information into useful knowledge. We shall translate this into accessible language so that popular movements can use it to develop alternative policies and give directives for action" (see Appendix 2).

nent. The same professional and technician strata that produces critical sectors also produces the public servants of technocratic organizations. Not all Brazilian technicians militate for technological autonomy; nor do they all become converted into the managers or the buyers of foreign technology. "Half our job is the buying of products, the other half is the selling," remarked, with a certain disenchantment, an electronics engineer from the University of Campinas.

The experience that some technicians have acquired in the course of the maturation process of the industry in which they work, has often led them to modify their evaluation of the role held by the state and the nature of the relations they maintain with it. This experience has led them to consider the state as a discontinuous entity where social negotiations are more or less possible. The Venezuelan engineers, regrouped in the Antonio José de Sucre Professional Movement (to which the majority of progressive engineers from the state telecommunications firms belong), reflected in 1976 on the attitude of professionals towards society and the state." We feel that the scientist and the technician can adopt a life style in which money would not be the be-all and end-all of success and in which practices—so widespread today—of administrative corruption and the distortion of values would be absent. We feel that the state enterprises, in an economic and social system that would give them a different role, can and must prove their technical and administrative efficiency. We feel, finally, that a scientific and technical development that responds to the real needs of each and everyone is possible" (Movimiento Antonio José de Sucre, 1976, p. 1).

When a computer engineer affirmed that "Brazilian industry should give preference, when possible to know-how developed in the country so that the integrating role that industry should have can be gradually confirmed," and when he added that "the state enterprises are particularly well placed to fulfil this role" (Da Costa Marques, 1975), he no doubt had in mind the famous precept of 19th century revolutionaries: "If the state is strong, it crushes us; if it is weak, we perish."

7. State Security

"Projects for public safety"

Whoever wishes information on the use made of information technologies by the repressive and military agencies Latin America would be better advised to consult the American Senate hearings than to go in quest of direct sources in the countries concerned. There is nothing odd in that.

As early as 1971, anyone who had followed the hearings of the Senate Sub-Committee for Western Hemisphere affairs (U.S. Senate, 1971) would have learned that the "Project for Public Safety," then applied in Brazil, had permitted the training, during the preceding years, of more than 100,000 Brazilian police agents and the sending of 523 officers to U.S. Police Academies. One could have learned that, also in the case of Brazil, the USAID (US Agency of International Development) had established its quarters in three institutions: the National Police Academy, the National Telecommunications Center, and the National Institute of Criminology and Identification. One of its priorities was the training of technicians in telecommunications and the construction, installation, and equiping of communication nodes to assure better contact between the states and between Brasilia and the federated states. These hearings also tell us what type of telecommunications material the United States offered Brazil between 1963 and 1969, hardware destined, according to witnesses and those directly concerned, "for the laying of the foundations of a national and interstate communication system, developing the communication capacity of portable radio for periods of civil strife and increasing the control efficiency of police patrols." In 1971, about 30 experts from the U.S. Police were detached to Brazil for the public security project. 80 Brazilian officers took courses at the International Police Academy in Washington.

By reading other hearings, one could also have been informed of other similar American aid programs, albeit more low key, being carried out in Central America, Uruguay, Venezuela, and elsewhere. These aid programs to the forces of repression are still evolving. A USAID official declared in 1975 that his agency now supplied computers only to Latin American police forces. An AID document, describing the aid given to the Venezuelan government, reveals that "the technical groundwork has been laid for the country's public safety agencies, processes through electronic data processing and related processes, to pool their identification and intelligence data in a central location for more efficient coordination and rapid distribution of relevant facts and leads." (See Nadel and Wiener, 1977, p. 26.)

According to another official, the computers came under agreements that had nothing to do with public security. In Chile, for example, in 1975–1976, a grant given for "agriculture" included, in fact, "a computer component." However, as an AID member admitted, the USAID has no means of controlling the eventual use of the computer which has been sent. "We are in a position similar to a car manufacturer," declared the director of information of IBM, the supplier of these computers, in order to remove all responsibility for possible uses of these machines from the shoulders of his firm." If General Motors sells you a car, and you use it to kill someone, that doesn't make General Motors responsible" (Nadel and Wiener, 1977, p. 23).

Police Internationale

These documents give a brief outline of the information technologies with which the repressive and military forces of Latin American countries are equipped. They do not enable one to perceive their real functioning in each country nor their articulation in an overall policy. Consulted on this point, official agencies prefer to sidestep any questions. The logic of the state secret, particularly in countries where the doctrine of national security is in effect, forbids the distribution of any information touching on this decisive segment of communication networks. It comes as no surprise that specialists and researchers in information science are manifesting their doubts, or even their perplexity, when this aspect of computer use is noted. And still, indications of the use of computers in systems of control and repression are increasing. Police patrol cars in Chile and Argentina are equipped with computer terminals. Under the military junta, anyone questioned in the street in Buenos Aires, had to produce a magnetic identity card which gave instantaneous information of that person's past history (Digicon system).

Several testimonies by political detainees in Chile and Argentina show the fluidity of the circulation of information on citizens between the police forces of these countries. The trade journal *Computer Decisions* reports the case of a clergyman, picked up for questioning on his arrival in Uruguay. During the interrogation "the police tried to get him to talk about a Catholic priest they were investigating." During this interrogation the police produced "a computer printout describing the details of the career of his colleague." It had all his successive addresses, his salary at each point in his career and his telephone numbers. The wanted priest was not a Uruguayan citizen and probably had never been in that country (Nadel and Wiener, 1977, p. 23). What is the role that the new technologies play in the control and repression of individuals? Taking the Latin American population as a whole, are the differences really significant between countries with authoritarian regimes and those with so-called liberal democracies? The domain of national security does not seem to respect levels of economic and political development. Brazil and the Dominican Republic obtained at almost the same time the most sophisticated technologies for computer control of passengers in airports.

The theme of national security remains a shadowy zone for social science research in Latin America.

Chapter 4

From the Computer Challenge to the Transnational Challenge

1. International Telematic Networks

A tentacle-like expansion

Eight types of global computer processing networks cover all parts of the world. They have laid the foundation for a transnational model of information circulation, this new multifaceted commodity. According to a study carried out for the Organization for Economic Cooperation and Development (OECD) by the firm Logica, the different applications of computer networks can be grouped in the following manner: 1) Coordination of production and distribution on an international scale for industrial firms; 2) Financial management of firms at an international level; 3) Processing of staff files and wage slips; 4) Movements of bank accounts and credit authorizations; 5) Reservations for airline companies and travel agencies; 6) Exchanges of statistical data between governments and administrations by means of private international networks; 7) Transmission of scientific and technical data between laboratories; 8) Control of the environment.[1]

In 1980, there were between 100 and 150 networks in these different categories. About 60 of these telecomputer networks were managed by private firms like CYBERNET, a network belonging to Control Data, which links 2000 cities all over the world; MARK III, a network of General Electric which links 600 firms in 25 countries; Société Internationale pour la Télécommunication Aéronautique (SITA), which numbers 200 members and maintains a worldwide network of telereservation of airline tickets throughout 118 countries; Society for Worldwide Interbank Financial Telecommunications (SWIFT), which we have already discussed, and MEDLARS (Medical Literature and Retrieval System), created in 1965 by the U.S. National Library of Medicine with five mil-

---

[1] See the report on international networks in *Le Monde Diplomatique* (1980, pp. 14–18).

TABLE 4.1. PRINCIPAL ON-LINE SERVICE CORPORATIONS, 1980

Name	Location	Number of Data Bases Offered[a]		
		Total	Of Which: Non-United States	Total Offered as percentage of Total Number of Data Bases
Lockheed Information Systems	USA	82	—	21
SDC Search Service	USA	56	—	14
Data Resource Inc.	USA	40	—	10
QL Systems Inc.	Canada	39	39	10
ADP Network Services Inc.	USA	25	—	6
IRS	Italy	23	6	6
Interactive Data Corporation	USA	22	—	6
BRS Inc.	USA	22	—	6
General Electric	USA	21	—	5
I.P. Sharp Associates	Canada	20	20	5
Interactive Market Systems Inc.	USA	12	—	3
U.S. National Library of Medicine	USA	12	—	3
Telmar Media Systems Inc.	USA	11	—	3
Others[b]		108	5	42
Total		542	70	

Source: Ruth M. Landau, Judith Wanger, and Mary C. Berger, ed. *Directory of Online Databases* (Santa Monica, Calif., Cuadra Associates, 1980).

[a]Access to an on-line data base can be offered by several on-line service corporations. The total number of data bases covered here is 398.

[b]Fifty-seven service corporations offer access to 10 or fewer on-line data bases.

lion pieces of data in its memory, making it one of the biggest scientific reference systems in the world. (Table 4.1 lists the largest on-line database companies.)

The transnational information industry

The twists and turns in the process of developing the transnational information industry at the end of the century can be seen by looking at these networks. Their history is relatively recent, originating in the shadow of grand military projects or public works schemes. The big automatized network, ARPANET (Advanced Research Project Agency) was the first, in 1964, under the auspices of the Pentagon, linking military research centers and universities. A sign of the times, ARPANET has been transformed since its takeover by the telecommunications manufacturer, General Telephone and Electronics (GTE) into Telenet, one of the two intercontinental publicly-accessible, value-added commercial networks. With Tymnet, Telenet constitutes the principal transnational computer-communications system specifically dedicated to commercial transborder data flow. It is also through a program stimulated by American public authorities that the aeronautics firm, Lockheed, is today owner of one of the two biggest data base complexes. With SDC (Systems Development Corporation), Lockheed controls three quarters of the European market and 60% of the U.S. market.

More recently, in March 1980, EURONET was inaugurated, established on the initiative of the Commission of the European Communities

FIGURE 4.1. NATIONAL NETWORKS INTERCONNECTION

NORTH AMERICA	WESTERN EUROPE	
US—TYMNET	SPAIN—RETD	EEC—EURONET
US—TELENET	FRANCE—TRANSPAC	SWEDEN—TELEPAK
CANADA—DATAPAC	FRG—DATEX-P	FINLAND—FINNPAK
CANADA—INFOSWITCH	NETHERLANDS—DATANET-1	NORWAY—NORPAK
MEXICO—SCT.	UK—PSS	SWITZERLAND—TELEPAC
INTERNATIONAL GATEWAYS	INTERNATIONAL GATEWAYS	
US—ITT, RCA, WUI, FTCC	PARIS—NTI LONDON—IPSS FRANKFURT	
CANADA—TELEGLOBE		

SOUTHEAST ASIA
INTERNATIONAL GATEWAYS
JAPAN—ICEA, VENUS—P AUSTRALIA—MIDAS NEW ZEALAND—OASIS
JAPAN—DXX-P

Source: EURONET Diane News, n. 26, April 1982.

by a consortium of the PTTs of the Community member countries. EURONET is thus an international public-switched data transmission network. Its main function is essentially to provide on-line access to machine-readable data bases within the European Community. Connections with other countries are in the process of being established (see Figure 4.1). A separate organization, DIANE (Direct Information Access Network) assures the recruitment of producers to be linked to the EURONET network.

The unequal sharing of information resources (in terms of databases) was as follows in 1982: the United States controlled 56% of databases, the EEC countries 26% and the remaining 18% was divided among the international organizations and the "rest of the world." American producers—almost half being private firms—owned five times the number of numeric databases as the EEC countries and had collected three and a half times as many bibliographic records (see Tables 4.2, 4.3, 4.4). When EURONET–DIANE inaugurated its network in 1980, Europe had only 50 bases: by 1982, it had 264.

It was only in 1980–1981 that some Latin American countries (with the exception of Venezuela) were connected to one of the two big American networks. Among them, Mexico, Chile, and Brazil have only just been integrated into them and are not listed, as yet, on published listings (see Figure 4.1).

In the race for the production and transmission of information, big

TABLE 4.2. DISTRIBUTION OF UNIQUE DATABASES PRODUCED BY ALL CATEGORIES OF PRODUCERS, ACCORDING TO ORIGIN OF PRODUCERS BY TYPE OF DATABASES (1982)

Origin of Producers	Type of Databases					All Categories of Data Bases
	Textual		Numerical			
	Biblio.	Factual	Mixed text/ Num.	Time series	Other numeric	
U.S.A.	155	83	105	140	87	570
EEC (CEC included)	113	71	21	29	30	264
Rest of the world	69	27	6	27	31	160
International organisations (CEC excluded)	8	3	2	16	3	32
All origins	345	184	134	212	151	1026

Source: Prepared by Serge Lustac of the CEC's Information Supply Unit in the Directorate General for Information Market and Innovation. *DIANE News,* July–August 1982.

TABLE 4.3. DISTRIBUTION OF BIBLIOGRAPHIC RECORDS PRODUCED ACCORDING TO ORIGIN OF PRODUCERS BY CATEGORY OF PRODUCERS (1982) (× 1.000.000 RECORDS)

Origin of Producers	Private Database Producers	Public or Non Profit Database Producers	All Categories of Producers
USA	33.2	41.9	75.1
EEC (CEC included)	4.9	16.3	21.2
Rest of the world	0.8	6.2	7.0
International organisations (CEC excluded)	—	1.5	1.5
All origins	38.9	65.9	104.8

Source: Prepared by Serge Lustac of the CEC's Information Supply Unit in the Directorate General for Information Market and Innovation. *DIANE News,* July–August 1982.

telematic groups and super-providers are emerging. IBM, AT&T, ITT, GTE, Xerox, and, particularly in Europe, the Thyssen group are attempting to share the industries of strategic and decision-making information, scientific knowledge, training, and entertainment.

The necessity of controlling all phases of the chain of electronic information services is stimulating new industrial and commercial configurations. Some are following a strategy of integration through the acquisition of missing links, from above by information providers and from below by producers, so as to control the whole chain of services from the creation of information to the supply to the user. This vertical integration is the case for producers of specialized information in online services, such as Mead Data, which controls the chain from produc-

TABLE 4.4. DISTRIBUTION OF TIME-SERIES PRODUCED ACCORDING TO ORIGIN OF PRODUCERS BY CATEGORY OF PRODUCERS (1982) (× 1.000.000 SERIES)

Origin of Producers	Private Database Producers	Public or Non Profit Database Producers	All Categories of Producers
USA	1.8	4.5	6.3
EEC (CEC included)	0.2	4.2	4.4
Rest of the world	0.1	0.5	0.6
International organisations	—	2.9	2.9
All origins	2.1	12.1	14.2

Source: Prepared by Serge Lustac of the CEC's Information Supply Unit in the Directorate General for Information Market and Innovation. *DIANE News,* July–August 1982.

tion, computer services, and transmission lines to the terminals for the bases of the LEXIS or NEXIS integral text. This vertical integration is also the case for the big publishers (McGraw-Hill and its recent acquisition, Data Resource (DRI), a famous macroeconomic data bank, Dow Jones, Dun & Bradstreet, Ziff Corporation), as well as the big financial groups (Citibank, Chase Econometric, American Express, etc.) and the managers or developers of the big telecommunications networks (AT&T, GTE-Telenet, IBM-SBS). The movement towards integration is completed by a movement of joint ventures or alliance strategies for sounding out as yet unreliable markets.

It is in this context that multiple actions to enmesh multiple systems of information distribution within the same enterprise are unfolding. Strategies of multimedia or multi-channel development are bringing together widely varying forms of hardware and software (for example, Warner-Amex, Westinghouse-Teleprompter, and many others).[2]

---

[2] See Footnote 1, Chapter 2.

2. Conflictual Connections

Teledetection

All of the natural characteristics of Latin American terrain are the object of permanent observation and evaluation through two satellite systems. The Landsat system, with its telecommanded sensors, observes natural resources. The other, composed of weather satellites, is devoted to weather prediction and the permanent study of the evolution of climatic conditions. The data, in the form of photo-images and magnetic tapes, communicated by the Landsat system, includes mining, agricultural, forestry, maritime, hydrologic, geographical, cartographic, urban, and ecological resources. They are processed in special pick-up stations which exist on Latin American territory only in Brazil (since 1975) and Argentina (since 1981). The other Latin American countries acquire information through "terrestrial image banks" attached to these stations or most frequently—directly from the United States from NASA which controls the Landsat system.

The weather satellites, which include Tiros-N, depend on NOAA (National Oceanic and Atmospheric Administration) based in the United States. Their images, sensed in the form of electrical impulses by cheap ground receivers, give a general survey of the atmospheric conditions for the whole of the Western hemisphere. The editor of the *International Exchange News* points out that "access to such technology, virtually free of charge, is changing the science of weather prediction in Latin America." He adds: "In an increasingly interdependent world, inadequate meteorological predictions in one country can result in food shortages, even financial panic, in another land far away" (Blair, 1981, p. 48). The following example confirms the statements of this journalist, as evidenced by the interest shown by the Peruvian government for weather satellites able to detect temperature changes in the ocean waters, like those occurring regularly at the Peruvian coast around Christmas time. This warm current, called "del Niño" (of the babe Jesus), leads to tem-

127

perature changes in the water which disrupt the ecosystem that produces the nutrients that form the basis of the Peruvian anchovy industry
which, at 12 million tons, is the biggest fishery in the world. The Peru-
vians thus have a crucial interest in knowing in advance the onset of this
current. "Other persons, as far away as Europe, Japan, and the United
States share their concern. In Europe, fish meal made from the anchovy
harvest is a vital element in livestock feed; in the United States, anchovy
fish meal is the nutritional mainstay of the poultry industry. "Del Niño"
drastically cuts the anchovy harvest driving up the price of fish meal and
substitute feed grains such as soybeans (a staple in the Japanese diet).
Thus thermal anomalies in the Eastern equatorial Pacific, observable
first only to the ever alert eye of a satellite, can have impact around the
world."

Like the weather satellites, the tele-detection mechanisms of the
Landsat system are active components of the world market. The journalist cited above also affirms, "that Landsat, once feared as an ever
vigilent 'spy-in-the-sky,' is today generally recognized through the developing world as a vehicle by which each nation can inventory and explore
its own natural resources." Bolivia, he adds, leads the world in applying
remote sensing technology to development projects. Thanks to data pur-
chased from Brazil and the United States, Brazilian and American analysts have discovered extremely rich deposits of lithium, potassium, and
iron. "Bolivia is realizing many times over the less than $10,000 spent
processing and analyzing the Landsat data. For $139 million dollars, it
has sold the rights to begin extracting the lithium to the Lithium Corporation of America. Much more revenue can be expected as lithium becomes more important on the world market because of the energy crisis.
Lithium is not only needed to produce electric batteries, but it also is vital
to making tritium, an element to be used in the fusion reactors of the
future" (Blair, 1981, pp. 51–52). (Table 4.5 provides information on
users of Landsat data.)

In the transnational era, the imperatives of the world market require the information system that is provided by satellites, in the same
way that this market needed the underwater cable during the last century. Moreno Fraginals, from whom we have quoted earlier, shows the
significance of the new information technology. "The problem of the
market is directly linked to information and the manifestations of distribution: lateness, acceleration, blockage, vagueness, and interference.
When powerful economic groups begin to monopolize certain key mechanisms for the obtaining processing and transporting of information,
this appropriation has a dialectical effect and confers on them more
economic power, and at the same time, more information" (Moreno
Fraginals, 1978, p. 29).

TABLE 4.5. USERS OF LANDSAT DATA, BY REGION AND USER GROUP, 1975–1980 (PERCENTAGE)

Year and Type of Data	Industry	Federal, State and Local Governments	Academia	Individuals	Non-United States	Total
Digital tape reproduction						
1975	27	32	25	1	15	100
1976	23	45	12	2	18	100
1977	32	31	10	1	26	100
1978	29	39	9	—	23	100
1979	25	25	14	2	34	100
1980	30	17	7	1	45	100
Photographic reproduction						
1975	23	21	14	9	24	100[a]
1976	17	39	11	7	26	100
1977	28	24	11	6	31	100
1978	19	26	9	5	41	100
1979	19	25	10	7	39	100
1980	18	23	10	6	43	100

Source: United States Department of the Interior, Geological Survey
[a]Including unidentified.

The universal availability of information on nature and natural resources offered today by satellites would seem to contradict the interpretation of Moreno Fraginals in respect to previous technologies. The truth, however, is that information in itself is insufficient. It is only useful to those with the means for using it. In other words, the type of information supplied is conditioned by a profile of usage; in this sense the value of the results drawn from it is not only economic, for it also gives an account of a particular conception of social priorities. The information given, for example, on the warm currents along the Peruvian coast is not primarily of value to the Peruvian fishermen, but to speculators on the world market. The value of lithium depends on its intrinsic value, but also on the interest of big consortiums to exploit it. Furthermore, this value fluctuates as it is affected by other information that Landsat supplies on other deposits and on decisions made by those with the power to exploit the data. This explains, perhaps, why the question of the ownership of satellites which supply information is important to the superpowers. The American Senator, Stevenson, remarking on the privileged place of the United States in this area, thanks to Landsat, expressed his fear of having to share it with others: "The French are going to sell stereoscopic images in several years time. We should feel very concerned about this. We could maintain our lead, but others are in the process of passing us by" (Chabreuil, 1980).

From financial networks to medical information

Taking into account the slight differences in the rate of change in each country, the financial and banking system of Latin America is gradually being linked to the SWIFT network. Argentina, Ecuador, Venezuela, Chile, and Mexico were connected between 1980 and 1981. It is not by chance that the Latin American country with the largest number of banks integrated into this network is Chile. Officials of the Association of Banks recognize that, in some cases, prestige counts more than the interests of clients or real needs. On the other hand, in Brazil, where the large number of international financial operations apparently justifies integration, certain dispositions of economic policy, including measures of protection for the new computer and terminal industry, have postponed until late 1983 the decision to incorporate in the system (SEI, 1982, pp. 44–45).

Venezuela offers another significant example. The project for integration into SWIFT was openly fought by the professional associations of CANTV (National Limited Company of Telephones of Venezuela) which holds the monopoly over the transmission of international communications. But the pressure exercized by the subsidiaries of American banks (already linked by computer to their mother companies), which finance for the most part the enormous external debt of Venezuela, finally carried the day (Sutz, 1982, p. 19).

Many Latin American countries are already connected to the MEDLARS system, which holds a monopoly over medical data banks. Brazil and Colombia illustrate the discussions and reflections to which entry into the system of data banks can give rise. The connection by Colombia to the Medlars system in 1980 resulted in a good deal of debate among the country's medical and scientific circles, bringing to the surface very different conceptions of the management of information and relations between national scientific information policies and the hegemony of data banks situated outside national territory.

A part of the medical profession defended the principle of connection without any reservations, as MEDLARS could be consulted each time there was a need for data. This position was backed up by two key arguments: the universality of scientific knowledge, and the cheapness of these information purchases. If, moreover, added MEDLARS defenders, we transfer all medical data accumulated in Colombia into this American data bank, we will have available a centralized system unique for the quality of its response to the whole of our demands.

The other part of the profession, while recognizing the undoubted value in being able to profit from the data offered by MEDLARS, demanded that the decision be the object of a debate in which the pros and cons could be weighed. The eventual entry into this system constituted, for opponents, an occasion to question the centrifugal schema of the American data bank, the organization of information and, as a consequence, research in Colombia. As an alternative, they proposed the creation of a national data bank which would gather together all the data available in the country, to which could be added the responses solicited from MEDLARS by Colombian doctors who felt the need to consult this international data bank. This would be without prejudicing the sending of all data collected in Colombia to MEDLARS for the benefit all of the world's medical profession. The polemics, it must be said, were marked by subjectivity, for as one Colombian observer remarked: "people are ready to pay anything for information when they know their lives depend on it."

This was not the first time that the Colombian medical profession had had the occasion of debating the blessings and ills of international cooperation. Such debates raged strongly during the 1960s and 1970s when, through the application of agreements signed with the Ford and Rockefeller Foundations and the Population Council, Colombia became a laboratory in which demographic policies destined for the whole of Latin America were tried out. These debates did not lead to unanimity. Among some, they reinforced the conviction that a growing participation in universal models was indispensable for solving national problems. Others maintained the idea that only a prior definition of national problems and needs could enable the country to rethink the way in which scientific problems were approached. Today, it is this same logic, giving priority to the "national," which is compelling, in determined fashion, an examination of the international data bank system and the need to construct one's own system.

Reflecting on the usefulness of data banks like MEDLARS, to which Brazil has been affiliated since 1973, a Brazilian scientist went so far as to speak of a "pseudo-transfer of technology." She describes thus an absorption of technology which leads to total dependence in respect to innovations produced overseas and which reduces the transfer to the acquisition of a "black box" which denies the purchaser all possibility of participating in the production or eventual modification of the imported product. To back up her argument, she quotes Wilfred Lancaster, one of the promoters of MEDLARS, who recognizes in drawing up a balance sheet of its activity, that: "Research teams must be sufficiently trained to make smooth absorption and adequate adaptation possible." For this Brazilian scientist, the ability to negotiate with the outside world exists only if constant research and development work can be carried out within the country. "In the case of a pseudo-transfer, absorption and distribution are very slow and uncertain. The possibility of contributing in useful time (i.e., before the information becomes obsolete) to the development of a national equivalent and to the indispensable assimilation of foreign and international information is, for all practical purposes, zero" (Guedes Batelho, 1976).

Another problem raised by international data banks and computer transfers in general is that of the language in which information is distributed. Specialists and directors of scientific or information policies have not always given enough attention to this problem, even though it is serious. English is tending to become the language used for data processing technology the world over. Certain data banks, for example those covering chemistry and medicine, are virtually reserved for those in the United States. Some would say that this phenomenon is irreversible and that one should accommodate oneself to it. This domination reinforces the position of English as the language of commercial exchange and publication. One monopoly leads to another and forces national researchers into the circuit of international publications, i.e., English language publications.

A study carried out at the request of Colciencias, the Colombian Centre for Scientific Research, showed the preference of national scientists for international journals. The credibility attached to the latter goes hand in hand with a negative opinion of local specialized journals (Fondation A. L. 2001, 1978).[3] This is no more than the repetition of what happens elsewhere. Scientists "feel" recognized when they are published in English language journals. The fact that one can find bilingual or English editions of scientific and technical journals in countries like Brazil or Mexico reinforces the tendency to publish in English.

This recourse to an accepted foreign language is itself becoming an essential means of being heard by policy makers. This is one of the principal findings of a recent study by two Brazilian researchers on the "determination and use of social sciences research among and by policy makers": "Foreign languages, although being a barrier for the understanding of research results are an asset to capture the attention of policy makers, since they contribute to legitimizing the researcher's work. Re-

---

[3] On linguistic dependence, see Mattelart (1983).

search results and reports published in foreign languages and in foreign countries enjoy more legitimacy than the ones written in Portuguese and published in Brazil, even when the content is the same. If both a Brazilian and a foreign version exist, chances of capturing the attention of policy makers increase because the latter legitimizes the former" (de Souza Costa Barros, 1980, p. 7).

A nationalist doctrine

In direct line from the debates on the "New International Information and Communication Order," the question of regulating transborder data flows (TDF) came to be a central issue in discussions over North-South relations. The IBI (Inter-Governmental Bureau for Informatics), whose headquarters is in Rome and which was founded soon after the Second World War on the initiative of UNESCO, is one of the best-known sites for these discussions. It only began, however, to make an impact in international discussions on informatics towards the end of the 1970s. Unfortunately, very few industrialized countries (an exception being France) belong to it.[4]

Brazil is undoubtedly one of the Third World countries to have produced the most developed doctrine on the question of transborder data flows. The primary recommendations of the Brazilian delegates to the IBI Congress in Rome in 1980 were:

1. Situate on national territory, the greatest possible quantity of information resources—computers, software, data banks, and human resources in the form of technicians and managers. TDF are envisaged as a problem which is as much cultural as it is economic.

2. Discourage the teleprocessing of data by computers situated outside the country. On the other hand, give priority to the implantation of local copies of data banks or favor the use of bases already existing in the country when they exist.

3. Apply a policy of examining activities concerning TDF case by case. The control of international telematic linkages is envisaged as an efficient instrument for the carrying out of a policy of orienting the behavior of transnational corporations on national territory. Authorizations are specific, always provisional. An extremely precise questionnaire has to be filled out by any transnational wishing to transmit data, indicating: present control of the company (shareholders); national and foreign firms in which the company participates; what telecommunications

---

[4] Italy and Spain (where a training center for developing countries has been created) also belong to the IBI.

FIGURE 4.2. MATRIX OF BRAZILIAN TRANSBORDER DATA FLOW POLICIES

| | | Category of on-line transborder data flows | |
		Corporate	Commercial
On-line use of transborder data flows	Data communications	Person-to-person communications are not restricted	Brazilian PTT only; co-operation agreements possible
	Data-base access	Copy of data base in Brazil, whenever reasonable	Encouraged, but in co-operation with Brazilian institutions, preferably with copy of data base in Brazil. If no local copy, services are provided by the PTT, although co-operation agreements are possible
	Data processing (incl. use of software)	Not favored abroad if reasonable local alternative exists	Not allowed abroad, except in exceptional circumstances.

Source: SEI, Brasilia, Brazil, 1982

resources the company wants to implement; a detailed explanation of the application objectives and how the facilities will be used; characteristics of the information to be transmitted; information about the technical, technological and operational resources that the company has or intends to buy or use, for implementing the application. (See also Figure 4.2.)

Companies like Control Data which seek timesharing activities have seen their authorizations refused for precise reasons: "This activity has a negative influence on our balance of payments. It will limit the development of national timesharing companies; this service could have an influence on the nascent national microcomputer industry; . . . there is a possible impact on efforts to stimulate national activity in the software domain" (*Le Monde Diplomatique*, December 1980, p. 16).

Taking up the old doctrine of the "free flow of information" and taking refuge in a "humanist" attitude, a representative of Control Data replied, at the IBI Rome Conference, to the spokesmen for the demands of Brazil and the Third World: "Usually when people talk about these developments, they talk about the technology itself—of mainframes, minis and micros; of fiber optics and computer satellite links; of memory capacity and transmission speed. But they often forget that the discussion of this technology is not about technology itself—it is about people and . . . their ability to communicate across the street, across the country and across the world" (McCarter, 1980).

Not wanting to be outdone, an IBM director went one better: "The problems of hunger, poverty and disease; the drive to eliminate illiteracy and to increase educational attainment among the literate; the need to identify, assess and manage resources are matters which all nations confront with greater or lesser urgency, and they provide fertile ground for international cooperation. Informatics has an obvious part to play in any such effort. It must be equally obvious, however, that (with respect to) these common concerns, no two nations can have exactly the same priorities or bring exactly the same capabilities to bear. For that reason, the role of informatics will vary significantly from nation to nation, and a national informatics policy model suited to the needs of one nation is bound to be an inexact fit for any other nation" (McCarter, 1980).

3. Culture's Name Is IBM

Light investments

"If, by any chance, all the microelectronics researchers in Brazil took the same airplane to go to a seminar and this airplane crashed, the country would be left without a single researcher in this field, for their present number is no more than 200. On the other hand, no airplane in the world is sufficiently big to accommodate all the researchers of just one of IBM's laboratories, the one in New York for example," remarked one of the most brilliant researchers in Brazil from the laboratory of digital electronics of the University of Campinas. This illustrates the gap between this transnational enterprise and any one of the countries of the subcontinent. All the more so when one considers that Brazil has more researchers in this field than any other Latin American country.

In 1980, IBM devoted 1,277 million dollars to research and development throughout the world. The second American firm, in order of importance, Digital Equipment, invested less than a fifth of this: 217 million dollars. The ten largest American computer firms had 73% of the total investments for research in this field. IBM alone was responsible for almost half of this. Its total income in 1981 was 24 billion dollars, representing 50% of the world's computer business. In comparison, all of the Japanese firms in the computer business controlled only 10 to 15% of the market. Another important difference was that 52.5% of IBM's sales were in foreign countries, whereas for the Japanese firm, Fujitsu, for example, this figure was barely 23% in 1980.[5] (See Table 4.6.)

According to a promotion brochure distributed by IBM in Brazil, its first factory in Brazil was installed in 1939 in the region of Benfica (Rio de Janeiro). This was the first IBM factory outside of the United States. A second factory was constructed in Sumaré in 1972. These two factories

---

[5] Statistics from *Datamation*, September 1981 and *Business Week*, 14 December 1981.

TABLE 4.6. TOP COMPUTERS AND
RELATED EQUIPMENT
MANUFACTURERS (1981)

Companies	DP Revenues in Millions U.S. $
I.B.M. (U.S.)	24,175
Digital Equipment (U.S.) .	3,198
Control Data (U.S.)	3,168
N.C.R. (U.S.)	3,050
Burroughs (U.S.)	2,875
Univac (U.S.)	2,707
Fujitsu (Japan)	1,910
Honeywell (U.S.)	1,800
Hewlett-Packard (U.S.) ...	1,785
CII-HB (France)	1,600

Source: Le Monde, (SICOB), 22 September 1982.

in Brazil, plus one in Mexico, constitute the industrial presence of IBM in Latin America. In addition there are two scientific centers in these two countries, plus several research projects in Argentina, Colombia, Peru, and Chile. Compared to the installations and the production of IBM in other parts of the world, its activities in Latin America are insignificant. Europe accounts for 38% of IBM's total revenue and the United States, 47%. The share of the Third World scarcely exceeds 5%. As for IBM installations, Europe alone has five laboratories, six scientific centers, and 14 factories.

Nevertheless, the spectre of IBM haunts the continent. The overwhelming superiority of this firm in the total number of large computers installed in Latin America and in the training of thousands of technicians, engineers, and managers is shown less in its production and sales than through the power it holds over the future markets and on the fixing of uses for the computer it commercializes.

No public or private organization in Latin America has shown as much interest as IBM in looking for possible ways in which computers can be used in the region and in finding the necessary personnel.

But a presence heavy with consequences

In publicizing its scientific programs in Brazil, IBM affirms that,

> the development of talent and the well-being of the community are the primary concerns of IBM-Brazil. This philosophy is that of our scientific programs which contribute to the development of the university and

scientific community and offer solutions to the largest social problems of this country. The object of the professional and scientific programs of IBM-Brazil is to aid the development of scientific and educational institutions to encourage the training of a skilled labor force, to develop science and technology in general, to accelerate the transfer and the divulging of know-how and know-why, and to make possible the development of projects and activities that improve the living standards of the Brazilian community.

Faithful to these principles, between 1974 and 1980, IBM distributed 520 scholarships to major universities, sponsored bringing about 30 lecturers to Brazilian higher education establishments, and assisted another 30 to enable them to participate in international congresses. IBM sponsored the participation of three teachers in the program entitled "Latin America Computing Science Workshop" and founded, within the framework of its cultural exchange program, the Study Center for the Processing of Information for Education. This center administers a number of programs which are available to teaching institutions so that students and teachers can become familiar with the computer as an instrument useful in their work.

The presence of IBM in the universities has existed for some time. The University of Chile, in 1967, was the first Latin American university to have an IBM 360 computer available. In 1981 in Peru, a small IBM scientific group worked with the National Engineering University of Lima for a community aid program. Its intention was to "compensate for the insufficiencies of higher education centers in the country." Each year, IBM selects from 3 to 9 students from among those with the highest records in final examination and provides them with grants for further studies.

The "scientific presence" program of IBM sponsors a wide variety of projects. In Peru, for example, in the field of agriculture, it sponsors research on the optimization of cultivation and the improvement of irrigation. In Chile, within the framework of an aid agreement signed with the Institute of Nutrition and Food Technology, it makes available a terminal connected to the most powerful computers of the country (*Informatica*, 1979a; Garcia Castro, 1980). In Brazil, these "scientific presence" programs range from the "Leviathan" project, which, working with the History Department of the University of Sao Paulo, is attempting to develop a methodology to determine keywords, to the "Gastro" project, which, in collaboration with the Catholic University of Rio de Janeiro, is seeking to shed light on "models of normality of the liver." Other projects include the development of information systems within the framework of a master's degree in administrations sciences; the

"Braille" project for the direct translation of texts for the blind; a project under the Secretary of State for Education in Rio to train technicians in data processing (3,500 people trained in 1981); the project "Mancha aureolada," which analyzes certain types of parasites; a project carried out in collaboration with the University of Campinas on hygiene and safety in working conditions; a project to study the resistance of materials; and, finally, the "Carta" project, in collaboration with the Directorate of Hydrography and Navigation for the automatic production of nautical maps.

A software laboratory

In Colombia, IBM has signed an agreement with the SER Institute (inter-disciplinary center of Independent Professionals, a body with considerable prestige in Colombia), for the creation of an inter-institutional systems laboratory. On this occasion, IBM gave the institute a 370/145 computer. IBM itself outlined the reasons that led it to this collaboration: "IBM Colombia, as part of the IBM Corporation, and within its philosophy of social responsibility—a philosophy which is an integral part of its principals and beliefs—has a permanent interest in scientific achievement and in the use of computer technology for the benefit of society. IBM Colombia, as an active member of the community and following its principles and beliefs, has been cooperating for the past 15 years with several Colombian universities that installed computers for the use of higher education in Colombia. It was precisely through this collaboration with Colombian universities that some of the SER researchers had the opportunity to begin their study of the uses and applications of the computer in scientific research" (SER/IBM, n.d.).

The project, inaugurated in 1979, was expected to last four years. Its objective is to determine the optimal use of computers in four areas: 1) *The administration of penal justice.* The SER had carried out, over several years, a series of studies on the factors causing the congestion of courts and the inequality of the judicial system in respect to defendants deprived of education and money. This research improved a system of administrative information, recording the movement of different cases to allow judges to program their activities and prosecutors to control the functioning of trials. 2) *Education.* The research aims at making up for the deficiency of information on the quality of teaching. The intent is to establish a system of measures of educational success, through the application of theoretical and practical knowledge tests covering different fields to representative samples of pupils from the Colombian school system. The use of the computer was thought to be necessary to develop and evaluate the tests and to analyze the results. 3) *Social Security.* These studies propose the development of statistical tools that will make it possible to predict the consequences of social security policies on the budgets of supervisory administrations. 4) *Health and nutrition.* Here the goal is to perfect a simulation model for sanitary planning and to develop a methodology that will make it possible to evaluate the impact of the national food and nutrition plan.

Another mode of harnessing social creativity

IBM in primary and secondary teaching, IBM in health, IBM in art, IBM in social security, IBM in justice. What does this omnipresence without apparent purpose signify? Why does this giant of cybernetic planning go to the trouble of pursuing philanthropic guerilla warfare in small nations?

"Solving problems; this, in short, is what characterizes the basic activity of IBM," one can read in IBM advertisements. It has almost become a slogan. But IBM, curiously enough, never defines the problems it is going to resolve; it only offers a methodology, implicit in the computerized solution it proposes. One thing is certain: IBM will never offer any other solution than a computerized one. Its reasoning is based on one prerequisite: the computer is the best solution for all problems, and IBM, more than any other firm in the world, is in the vanguard of this type of solution.

When IBM becomes interested in a social problem, it is also interested in a future market; a captive one because the solutions proposed are necessarily linked to computers. But that is not all. When it "teaches" the use of these machines for the solution of problems, it also develops software that it can then sell to other customers with similar "problems."

The search for software, which gives a *raison d'être* to the machine by allowing it to solve a problem, creates a redeployment of social connections between the hardware manufacturer and the individuals and social groups which contribute their intellectual raw material. The search for solutions becomes a pious adventure of creativity extraction for the firm, within the limits imposed by a "final solution," over which it has control.

The "IBM solution" to problems requires an alliance with intellectuals and creators and the constitution of think-tanks from which the firm can draw for software innovation which will allow the formation of a social use for its technology. Without realizing it, perhaps, the manager of university programs for IBM-Argentina said exactly this at the 8th Latin American Conference on Informatics, by insisting on the pressing need to create new software able to stretch the social use of computer systems to the utmost.

Unaware of the needs of man in this area, our professional progress is very slow when we examine the problem of future man-machine integration. We have been able to make toys which work with television sets. We know how to make very amusing things. Nevertheless, this technology would be better applied to education where our development is very slow. Why? Because we do not know the human being. We do not know how to use this technology so that one can learn more easily. In my opinion, this is where we hit the nail on the head in respect to our principal problems. I also believe that it is in this area that we can expect to have the greatest influence. We must not forget that it is in everyday life that the greatest impact of our technology will be felt. (*Clarin*, 1981)[6]

Commenting on the recent entry of IBM into the microcomputer market, a French journalist noted: "IBM has the reputation of carrying a great deal of weight in computers. This reputation is exaggerated, but the decisions of the American giant still have a driving force which multiplies their impact" (Arvonny, 1981). This remark is particularly appropriate in Latin America, where IBM seems to have taken over from all the other international organizations in prospecting for markets and in offering solutions. The search for solutions through the market fits in very well with the political winds blowing in this part of the world at this time; the neo-liberal model is systematically pushing states to turn over their their public functions to the private sector.

Times have changed. The 1960s saw the peak of a wave of studies and social experiments financed by the Ford and Rockefeller foundations, American universities and organizations directly linked to the US government, like the U.S. Agency for International Development (USAID), or of projects like the Alliance for Progress or, again, the Peace Corps. All of these official actors of U.S. aid programs, during this period, set themselves to finding a social use for television technologies, serving as a vanguard in the creation of markets. The decade which began in 1980, and which places private enterprise as the principal actor of development, will no doubt see the flourishing of new mechanisms— less closely identifiable with political power—of capturing economic and cultural markets with the private firm becoming its own prospector.

The Colombian case provides more important information (see Jaramillo, 1979). No other Latin American country in the last 20 years has been presented with such a large number of projects, all aimed at trying

---

[6] Argentina is undoubtedly the Latin American country where computer applications in teaching are the most advanced. At the beginning of 1982, Brazil underwrote, with Argentina, a cooperation and aid plan in this field. (For a debate on educational software, see Appendix 3.)

to find new applications for audiovisual technology in education—from the satellite to television. The numerous debates by diverse sectors of Colombian society during the 1968–1973 period led to the failure of these electronic "solutions." Such was the case of the CAVISAT project which was presented as a technological panacea. Ten years after the failure of educational television, data processing technology, wrapped in the aseptic packaging of limited liability companies, is promoted as a new miracle solution to social problems. Previous debates at least made possible the development of a consciousness over something that transnationals would prefer to see forgotten: technology does not fall into a social vacuum.

Prospects

Human Rights and the Rights of Peoples

1. View from the South: Give Hidden Facts Their Political Sense

Traveling through Latin America in order to try to define the way in which it is submitting to the new technologies makes one reflect on themes that should mark the future of its peoples and the history of its institutions. Questions long repressed and put off are returning in force and stubbornly imposing themselves. New situations and new ways of conceiving of change define new priorities.

Through analyses which cover again paths already covered or which attempt to unearth new theoretical perspectives, through the simple description of situations or the testimonies of those who are their actors, we have tried, throughout this book, to reveal the essential characteristics of the transformations occurring in the dominant model of communication, as well as the viewpoints and social demands that could underlie an alternative. At the end of this study, one conclusion imposes itself: if technological changes tend to modify the political horizon radically, at the same time this horizon is certainly the place where the decisions must be taken and the final meaning of these innovations is to be found. This prevents one from envisaging—and worse still accepting—technological expansion as the agent of an a-historical fatalism.

In the age of telematic choices, Latin America is at the crossroads. Some themes can no longer be avoided.

The stakes of decentralization

The model of implantation of computer technologies in Latin America reinforces the tendency to the growing centralization of economic and institutional decisions. The prophets of the computerized society, following the example of promoters and decision-makers, repeat, nevertheless, like a leitmotiv, the contrary: computerization is leading to decentralization. This is the opinion of the president of TELEBRAS:

"Industrial decentralization, de-urbanization, energy savings, all of this is only possible thanks to telecommunications and computers. These are the only means capable of offering man an escape outlet from the cruelty of megatropolises and of supplying him with the elements necessary for making decisions from a distance" (*Revista Nacional de Telecomunicações*, September 1, 1979, p. 70).

Meanwhile, the evidence at hand indicates that computerization processes are presently linked to social uses which lead in the direction of a reinforcement of the capacity for economic concentration of large firms and their potential for control over citizens. There is thus a strong tendency for the concentration of the means of mass communication in the preparatory stage of the introduction of new technologies; the computerization of banking and financial services as instruments of monopolization; identity controls through magnetic cards; new strategies of repression; finally, microcomputers (symbols of the promised decentralization) are primarily destined for large industrial and financial firms. The Brazilian videotex system, videocassette recorders in Caracas, or the new digitial telephone centers in Chile only reinforce the privileges of certain social categories.

A director of the Sao Paulo videotex system explained in July 1981: "The user aimed at by the videotex terminal belongs to a specific fringe of the population, and to certain advanced firms, those which have the most need of the information proposed. Individuals participating in the experiment are chosen from among those with a telephone which, in Brazil, already represents a selection of those with high incomes." This approach was confirmed in September 1982 by one of the most fervent proponents of the Giscardian policy of exporting the "French telematic solution": "In the same way that money makes money, technology makes technology. Those who make use of advanced technology today have more chance of being even richer in advanced technology in five or ten years time" (Thery, 1982).

The case of videotex is particularly attractive because its technological structure is at the root of all models of decentralization and participation, which are cited as such by proponents of the system. But facts are stubborn. The Velizy videotex experiment, one of the most advanced in Europe, and which inspired the Brazilian project, has not been spared by critics, who have not missed the occasion of underlining the difficulty of bypassing the marketing model. "The Velizy experiment enables one to judge this system in action: producers of information, essentially administrations and firms with considerable means (railways, chain-stores, etc.) use videotex to present a catalog of their services and its interactivity for immediate on-line commercial operations (purchase of an article, reservations, etc.) . . . . As for the public, it remains enclosed within a classic relation to information, its needs only taken into consideration by a permanent marketing study . . . Telematics is only socially justified if its interactive potential is exploited. This implies active users, escaping from the exclusive role of consumer within which commercial firms and administrations have so far confined them" (Festinger and Joxe, 1982).

If some have complained of the absence of the associative sector in experiments like that of Velizy and the social segregation that they reproduce, how can one not think that these defaults can only be enlarged in situations like that of Brazil with its enormous social antagonisms and its legal obstacles to the organization of the popular classes?

What is lacking, and it is normal that it should be so, for it is completely foreign to the conception of society that inspires this type of decentralization, is the possibility for the individual to participate in the development of the ground rules that govern this decentralization. The type of technology to be adopted is not, however, a subject of discussion. The question that is not asked is whether the computer is really the solution to any existing problem at any given moment. In the last analysis, the real participation of the different components of civil society in the definition of the social uses of these technologies is not encouraged. Promoted as if they were intrinsically interactive and as if they necessarily made participation easier, the incorporation of these technologies is being carried out under the keynote of non-interactivity.

Through a model advertising decentralization as a form of social participation, the state is redefining itself in its totality and, at the same time, the relation of private enterprise with the national and international situation into which it fits is also being redefined. By means of this decentralization, the state is secreting new forms of legitimization of its central authority, while feigning to withdraw from the game. In business enterprise, this type of decentralization is bringing new, less conflictive modes of work organization and original paths of market penetration, as well as multiplying its possibilities of appropriating the creative potential of individuals and social groups. This decentralization through the market, this booby-trapped participation is, in reality, leading to the atomization of society which is disintegrating forms of community life and collective power by proposing a new culture founded on an extreme individualism.

The decentralization project promoted by the logic of transnational power, with the concrete forms it assumes in each nation, supports various publicized social demands which differ substantially from what is being proposed. The actions of various social sectors which demand participation, in terms of their own perspectives, in the construction of a project for society, receive in response the offer of a decentralization which rules out the possibility of other options. The notion of decentralization and, even more, that of participation are becoming areas of social confrontation. Given that systems of information have become one of the poles of the restructuring of institutions, no discussion of these systems can avoid a detour through these concepts. The decentralization-atomization which is opposed to decentralization as a corollary of democratic practice is redistributing the axes around which social alliances are being reconstituted.

The order of priorities

When one broaches the problems raised by the advent of new information technologies, one often comes up against a certain scepticism as to the real importance of this question for Latin America. One frequently faces the argument that problems of hunger, illiteracy, or health are so grave on this continent that all forces aspiring to the suppression of injustice and inequality must, above all, devote themselves to solving this situation of immediate distress. This reasoning insinuates that questions concerning technological changes are, for the moment, the exclusive property of highly industrialized countries. To import them into Latin America, is to graft a problem of the central countries onto the periphery which is far removed from it. In this perspective, all reflection on the arrival of these new technologies appears as a diversionary maneuver.

The arguments that are stressed in order to prevent discussion of the sociocultural effects of new technologies present at least two flaws. First, as we have seen, the introduction of computers into Latin America is not a problem for tomorrow but the reality of today, a present that promises the future. The second flaw comes from a series of misunderstandings which can only be explained in terms of a way of conceiving the world, and, in consequence, of acting on it. This reasoning rests on the idea that social processes can be fragmented into discontinuous units and that the opportune moment for discussing certain themes and questions is subject to the emergence of new economic conditions. One could minimize the impact of this viewpoint, if the recent history of Latin America and other regions of the world did not offer tragic examples of the consequences of such a conception. Not only has the construction of truly democratic societies failed, but, moreover, for not having posed problems on the margin of economic immediacy, one has not even been able to resolve economic problems themselves with any efficiency. The limits of a simple-minded economism prevent it from seeing the technological phenomenon as a structural element of an economic, political, and cultural model of development. As information systems become more and more modernized, discontent with the technological variable sharpens and the impasses of a certain type of economic thought appear (as illustration see Emmanuel, 1981).

Obviously, this does not mean that we wish to conceal the tragic situation in which a large part of the population in Latin America lives, nor are we unaware that an analysis of general problems must be made from a perspective which takes into account the historical, cultural, and social particularities of the continent.

The internationalization of telematics, founded on the logic of a new division of labor and the characteristics of the world market, pose problems in Latin America that are similar to those formulated in the central countries. It is not by chance that discussions within the Intergovernmental Bureau for Informatics (IBI) on transborder data flows have put European and Latin American countries on equal terms, whereas they were dissociated during the debates on the New International Information Order at UNESCO.[1] It is symptomatic that Latin America has already succeeded in forming the first regional association on computer policies, the Latin American Conference of Information Officials (CALAI), whereas it could not entirely overcome the difficulties of creating a Latin American press agency.

Human rights

The question of transborder data flows, which comes back to the right of nations to decide the use of their informational heritage, coexists on the international scene with that of the rights of the individual to decide which information affects the right to privacy. The risk of a concentration of information on each citizen which the development of computers and telecommunications heralds, forces one to carefully consider the problem in each country. Discussion can, therefore, neither be avoided, nor transposed solely onto the level of international relations. For a long time, international debate on communication has been dominated by the

---

[1] We should qualify these statements. Day after day, we see, in effect, that all the European countries do not have the same way of envisaging the struggle against American hegemony in this domain. In fact, despite certain contradictions, France is one of the most coherent sites of resistance to American networks. On the other hand, countries like Great Britain have transformed themselves into veritable bridgeheads for the internationalization of telematic networks along the lines of the American model.

In 1980, 66% of data flows between Western Europe and the United States originated in Great Britain. Transatlantic information flows represent two thirds of British transborder flows. In the other European countries, this does not exceed 10%. Great Britain remains faithful to its role of trampoline for a certain model of implantation of the new communications technologies, as has been the case for the videocassette recorder, the videodisc, and, more recently, optical fibers and satellites.

idea—supported by numerous Third World countries—that the major problem was the disequilibrium of information flows and that the responsibility for this state of affairs fell mainly on the dominant countries. In the name of this priority, a thorough analysis of each internal situation was postponed. In the name of a consensus which scarcely troubled itself with details and which homogenized states with diametrically opposed conceptions of the individual in society, it did not appear necessary to examine the place of the citizen, ordinary consumer of the information generated most often at the headquarters of some transnational press agency. And yet this ultimate link in the chain should have been the point of departure for all discussion.

The concept of decentralization-atomization is once again opposed to that of democratic decentralization when it comes to defining the place of the individual in society. The essential tropism of the former is to consider the individual like an isolated cell, whose interests coincide with those of other individuals through the market place. The second perceives the individual as a subjectivity to respect, in the context of a collective identity, for participating in the search for common solutions.

These two contradictory views lead to two equally contradictory approaches to the notion of privacy. This question takes on a singular shape in Latin America, because in this part of the world, the defense of privacy evokes situations much more harrowing than in other countries. For a large number of Latin American citizens, the question is not only the accumulation of information in a computer used to decide the granting or the refusal of bank credit, contrary to the opinion of the President of the Chilean ECOM:

"For us," he argued in the course of an interview, "all personal information is confidential . . . . The problem has arisen in Chile in connection with the information we handle over credit cards. Those who are incorporated into the credit card system confess. Through their repeated transactions, they confess what they are doing, where they go, their private life, what they buy, what interests them. All this is a part of personal information" (*La Tercera de la Hora*, 1981).

In Latin America, the argument of "national security" regularly intervenes to point out the demarcation line between what is forbidden and what is permitted, between what one can say and what one must remain silent about, between what defines the domain of privacy and is thus the heritage of every citizen and what is in the public domain and thus the jurisdiction of the state. The reflections of the director of the journal *Revista Nacional de Telecommunicação* throw some light on this point and their value certainly transcends the limits of the Brazilian case: "In a country where the word privacy is not in the dictionary, what can one hope for in respect of the private life of its citizens? . . . . It is not only technology which menaces the Brazilian citizen. It is perhaps only the most dangerous and sophisticated form of menace for the years to come . . . . The secrecy of information is daily violated even by fifth grade public servants and subaltern police officers. This may be over the telephone, in the mail, in the absurd harassments of an underdeveloped bureaucracy, in the famous credit protection services, in the main data banks, in income tax, in the banking system, in medical consulting rooms, at reception areas of administrative services which continue to be unaware of the legal banning of the retention of identity papers . . . In the face of all this, the Brazilian seems to be still unconscious and un-prepared. He does not take seriously, nor does he fear, the risks that technology represents, in particular computers and telecommunications, in these days of fantastic microcircuits and microcomputers" (Siqueira, 1979).

Computerization and social movements

The recent eruption of a theme like the right to use information about individuals and nations has helped make necessary the redefinition of the bases on which international relations are founded. This need coincides with the willingness shown by various components of social movements to pose for themselves again the question of the role of different groups and classes in the transformation of society. In the same perspective, the need to reconsider the place of the individual within these movements and the space of the individual (and of subjectivity) in relation to the collective is also affirmed. Other social demands have today been added to the historical forms of action and resistance of the popular classes. Through their specificity,[2] these new movements show the variety of interests seeking to integrate the plurality of everyday life into politics. The multiplication of social movements, the struggle for the safeguarding of cultural autonomy are growing in importance, faced with the process of computerization which tends to suppress differences.

The modifications of the production process, the logical result of technological innovations linked to computers, is launching new challenges to professional organizations and trade unions. The changes in the internal composition of the working class, the realities of delocalized work and the shift in the social function of technicians and professionals

---

[2] See, for example, the dossier on "Le réveil des Indiens d'Amérique Latine", *Le Monde Diplomatique*, March 1982 and the numerous articles and dossiers published by *Amérique Latine*, journal of the Centre de recherche sur l'Amérique Latine et le Tiers-monde (CETRAL), Paris.

have, in certain industrialized countries, given notice to union organizations to redefine their mode of action and their role in relation to other social movements. Unions today find themselves faced with entirely unforeseen situations which force them to rethink their actions and the very nature of their function. To confine themselves to a corporatist logic which limits them to dispersed conflicts and the defense of the *status quo* runs the risk of marginalizing the union and making it lose its role as social representative. The new option open to it is take account of the transformations brought about by new technologies and to attempt new forms of intervention and control, not only within the factory, but also within the social space where it is inscribed.

The advance of new information technologies has not yet, admittedly, provoked changes in Latin America on the scale of those that the union movement in Western countries is, or is not, preparing to confront. Latin America finds itself, however, faced with the first consequences of these innovations. According to some observers (Rada, 1981b), most Latin American trade unions are not yet concerned with these consequences. The fact that, for the first time, the Mexican Telephonists' Union refers to the new technologies in its demands, is a first sign of awakening. Other signs are the concern shown by Venezuelan journalists over the modernization of press firms and the action of Brazilian computer scientists in alerting other union organizations in the country, which have been extremely slow to take up these new challenges.

Along with the process of the institutionalization of computers in Latin America, messianic ideas are flourishing: the virtual non-cost of information, the power of information, the interdependence that it creates. The logic underlying these ideas is faultless. They offer the world the promise of a freedom without restriction, the freedom of choice and decision. In effect, if information were free, everyone could have access to it. If information gave power, and were within the grasp of everyone, then power would be in the hands of everyone. If the planetarization of information engendered interdependence, then there would no longer be any risk that power could be used by some to dominate others.

Reality reveals what the myth veils. It is through the conflicts of social actors that the use values of information emerge.

2. View from the North: Construct a Field of Research-Action[3]

No one can ignore that in a country like France (or any large industrialized country in Europe) the imperative of reconquering the internal market by communication technologies can conflict with the need to take into account "social demand," in other words, the need to involve those concerned in technological choices. In parallel fashion, no one can ignore that the imperative of conquering external markets by communication technologies can conflict with the need to find new forms of cooperation and association between North and South.

This is an essential contradiction that one must be honest enough to recognize when one struggles, within the present framework of so-called international constraints, against the imbalances between North and South and when one seeks to give impetus to a policy of research on transfers of communications technology which is coherent with this idea. How can one give form to the desire formulated by President Mitterrand at Versailles in respect to technology transfers?: "If it is in the interest of the industrialized countries that the immense market of the countries of the South is opened up to technological revolution; science and technology must bring to these countries conditions of survival and dignity by protecting and mobilizing their natural resources and their environment."

As we have already remarked, any model for overcoming the crisis through high technology necessarily requires schemas of international alliances, which reinforce contradictory interrelations between the big industrialized countries. Priority to the conquest of the American mar-

---

[3] Extracted from the final Report "Mission Technologie, Diffusion de la Culture et Communication" (under the presidence of A. Mattelart and Y. Stourdze), Paris, 1982, Ministry of Research and Industry. (See Mattelart and Stourdze, 1982.)

ket, tendency to repatriate factories from the Third World because of automation, dissension within the EEC in the construction of the "industrial unity" of the old continent in the face of the Japanese and American menace, as is evidenced by the merger between AT&T and Philips, difficulties to propose to the countries of the South a new type of alliance with what would be the "European alternative"; these are the many structural interferences which, if we are not careful, could reduce to nothing the best of intentions.

This being the case, what kind of research is needed to contribute to the progressive resolution of, what remains and will long remain, a major challenge to the redefinition of relations between the well-to-do and the impoverished?

• *Research which dares to pose the same questions on "social demand" as those posed by critical research-action in the North on the insertion of the new technologies.* The growing presence of large French telecommunications and telematic firms in Third World markets forces us to question the practices of these firms, for the most part nationalized, in comparison with Japanese, American, German, Swedish, or Dutch transnationals.

For the attentive observer of the external approaches of these French firms, it is only too obvious that the empiricist and blow-by-blow approach has, in the majority of cases, been the dominant norm. The weakness of reflection, as much at the level of the technical training offered by state institutions (such as the services of the Direction Générale des Télécommunications) or public enterprises to Third World countries, as at the level of the knowledge of the social terrain in which these firms and institutions invest or export their products and services, can only be understood in terms of the deficiencies of the economic and social research systems of these firms and institutions and similar deficiencies in university critical research.

The question is extremely concrete: how can we arrange it so that French firms proposing videotex services and products (as is the case today in Brazil) no longer limit themselves to selling material while ignoring the probable social uses?

• *Research which attempts to provoke the coming together of groups and individuals who contribute towards the expansion of spaces of liberty in countries where the forces of change are not in government and where the vast majority are constrained to pursue their task in conditions of exclusion or even harassment and repression.* The only way of developing a policy which responds to the aspirations and the real needs of the peoples of the Third World is through an effective dialogue with interlocutors genuinely engaged in change; a dialogue based on the necessity of knowing each other and the will to meet together to explore the possibilities for cooperation; a relation between equals which shares the same faith in freedom, justice, and democracy.

Research, because of the plurality of partners involved, is a privileged domain where it is possible to begin to construct with other interlocutors of the Third World a new type of cooperation policy. A new approach for an analysis of the social and cultural impact of the new technologies that the industrialized core-countries export or transfer to the Third World is outlined in *relations between constantly changing civil societies, from one civil society to another.* International research projects must seek support from non-governmental organizations, the union movement, the women's movement, professional and scientific associations, etc.

• *Research which does not limit itself to accompanying or preceding the exportation of technology by large firms and institutions but which makes available to Third World countries all existing information on experiments in democratic communication in the North countries, and all the results of these "social experiments" which aim to associate local collectivities, secondary school pupils or other organizations of civil society in the determination of their own model of communication.* The example of Mozambique, drawing the democratic lessons from Italian experiments and preferring to import the light technologies used by the free radios and televisions in Italy in order not to fall into the centralizing clutches of the big audiovisual manufacturers, clearly illustrates the latent need felt by certain Third World countries for a self-reliant and self-managed development following the example of multiple groups of peasants, workers, women, or intellectuals whose reflection on the stake of the new technologies is surely more advanced than in the laboratories of the big electronics firms.

From this observation is born another requirement: that of knowing more about the many experiments in the construction of popular networks which are being developed in the Third World. For if the Third World is a demander of information on the situation in the developed world, it is not always the case that the latter takes an interest in the Third World. This self-important ignorance, worthy of a hopeless provincialism, has repercussions on the comprehension of the great international challenges of the time and the strategies proposed in response.

Concerned that a Japanese or American telematic transnationalization could signify the loss of its sovereignty and independence, France is also a country which belongs to the club of hegemonic nations. It is in reference to this position of France that Third World countries demand of the Agence France-Presse (AFP), the fourth press agency in the world, another behavior, another attitude towards them. Here again, the field of research is strategic. If there exist a few—too few—studies on the nature of the information transmitted by this agency, there is practically no circulation of this research in professional circles. And yet, one notes, on the part of some journalists, a real demand for approaching their own craft and that of their institution in terms different from those based on the dominant belief according to which only a professional code of ethics can guarantee free and correct information. To reap this demand and transform it into a pedagogical research-action appears, in a France which is attempting to associate itself with a "new international information order," as a priority task.

Appendices

Appendix 1. Declaration of Mexico on Informatics, Development, and Peace (1981)*

1. In the course of the 60s and the 70s important technological advances were made in the field of electronics which have given a new dimension to informatics and its use in economic and social development. The use of these new techniques in informatics and telecommunications for the widening of knowledge, the improvement of management and the increase of productivity creates a new and important factor of disequilibrium between developed and developing countries. The decade of the 80s is a period of challenge and contradictions. On the one hand, science has greatly extended our understanding of the world and of society while a burgeoning of technology offers enormous possibilities for improving the standard of living and quality of life of all people. On the other hand, mankind is faced with increasingly complex problems which may condition its survival. These trends are interacting in a way which increases tensions within and between societies to the point of endangering peace. Informatics can play a critical role in lowering these tensions.

2. Among the problems raised are: the deadlock of the North-South dialogue; growing economic and technological disparities; widespread poverty, hunger, ignorance and disease; the arms race; the inadequacy of current approaches to development; the inability to fully master and effectively harness this great potential of science and technology for a substantial improvement in the conditions of life; and the quantitative and qualitative waste of human resources.

3. Recent technological breakthroughs and others which are expected are creating unprecedented opportunities for the betterment of

---

* Meeting organized under the auspices of IBI (June, 1981).

the human condition, but portend as well negative trends which need to be in almost all sectors of human activity, offers a powerful tool for the management of technological development, and opens up new possibilities for cultural and educational development. Herein lies the challenge: wisely used with humanitarian understanding it can contribute greatly to the solution of fundamental problems and hence to the establishment of peace. Applied in a technocratic and excessively centralized manner, it can increase the complexity of problems, rendering them more difficult to solve. Informatics is thus becoming more and more an instrument of power which affects the political, economic, social and cultural sphere nationally and worldwide and hence is of immediate concern to decision-makers at all levels.

4. One of the important consequences of these changes will be a redistribution of productive and service facilities on a worldwide basis which will pose a series of complex issues for Third World industrialization and development, thus calling for urgent consideration. Among other things, international debates are needed on transborder data flows and their impact on the international division of labour and technological concentration.

5. Informatics is an important ingredient as well as a consequence of development. Its mastering implies an endogenous and autonomous approach to development, an increasing reliance on human resource, a greater emphasis on its scientific and technological dimensions and an awareness of the implication for cultural identity and diversity. Informatics, to the extent it could become an effective instrument for promoting organizational, managerial and administrative structures, can assist in the solution of problems of development.

6. Due to the fact that many areas of informatics require extensive technological and economic resources it is important that a greater coordination and integration is effected at sub-regional and regional level.

7. The capacity to assimilate and evolve technology depends on the political will to adopt national strategies and policies and enhance international cooperation, permitting the development of adequate capacities and infrastructures for technology and management and of high quality training facilities.

8. Effective use of informatics requires the mastering of the capacity to generate and process information. The most important element in this respect is not only the tool itself but also the content of the information and the economic and socio-cultural context which conditions its receptivity and relevance.

9. The traditional forms of regional and international cooperation are insufficiently flexible and imaginative to meet the new needs. Hence new forms of cooperation must be urgently devised so as to ensure greater participation and enable the anticipation of problems before they arise.

10. The right to information, such as it is recognised by the Universal Declaration of Human Rights and international treaties, has acquired, due to technological evolution, a scope which is qualitatively and quantitatively different from that which prevailed when they were adopted. The concept of the "right to information" needs to be reinterpreted in the light of changes due to informatics.

11. Informatics, if developed in the interest of all of mankind, can serve as an instrument of emancipation and development fully preserving the right of individuals to privacy and self-fulfillment. Only thus can it effectively contribute to universal prosperity, human dignity, social justice and ultimately to world peace. The World Conference on Strategies and Policies for Informatics (SPIN II) to be held in Havana, Cuba, in June 1983 offers a propitious occasion for the promotion of the objectives set out in the present Declaration.

Appendix 2. An Innovative Service for the Popular Movements: The Brazilian Institute of Social and Economic Analyses (IBASE)

In recent years, the emergence of Brazilian popular movements has been characterized by unique depth and strength. Today, the diverse forms of popular organization, the growing awareness of relevant social problems and their causes, and the search for alternative paths can be seen throughout the country under the leadership of labor unions, professional and neighborhood associations as well as urban and rural grassroots communities.

These popular organizations, however, are confronted by a highly centralized, modernized and internationalized system of domination which poses new challenges to the development of truly popular participation processes. In the last 17 years of authoritarian regime, centralization of economic, political and cultural power was equalled by the capacity to produce distorted images of reality, under the disguise of modernization and new technologies, through control and manipulation of the media. In this context, the people face a sophisticated 'manufactured' system of information that conveys a biased version of reality. Direct knowledge of reality therefore becomes atomized at the grass roots and centralized at the level of the country's ruling elite, making reliable and updated information the privilege of a few.

Some initiatives to generate alternative information and analysis have been recently observed in universities and research centers; likewise, other regional and local institutions have developed valuable research and communication activities. Most of these initiatives, however, are limited largely by: (a) institutional constraints; (b) regional or local character of their initiatives; (c) lack of resources and specialization; and (d) absence of effective articulation with the grass roots, capable of unifying, generalizing and transmitting alternative knowledge on a national

162

scale. An added constraint is the relative distance of these centers from the direct actors of the social transformation; this distance results from both the structural limits of these institutions and from their elitist behavior in that which concerns popular movements.

General objectives of IBASE

IBASE's main objective is to provide an effective service of support and consultancy to the popular movements, including the organization of voluntary working groups of technicians and the implementation of a data bank strictly at the service and according to the expressed needs of popular organizations—grass-roots communities, churches, trade-unions, neighborhood associations, and so on. The originality of this initiative lies in its method of collecting socio-economic information not only from official sources and the media, but also by popular groups. As well as articulating elaboration of data-based reports and analyses with the expressed requests of popular organizations. Reliable information is thus transformed into usable knowledge for alternative policy formulation by popular organizations. In this way, IBASE is an attempt to (a) break the monopoly of socio-economic information, and (b) to help transform this information from an instrument of domination into a tool for achieving a participatory, democratic, self-reliant development.

Origins of IBASE

IBASE formally initiated its activities as a non-profit, non-partisan, independent institution in January 1981. The IBASE project emerged from several seminars, consultations and discussions in Brazil and abroad which began in mid-1979. In February 1980, IBASE's program proposals were presented to and discussed by the 15 participants of the Itaici meeting of the National Conference of Bishops of Brazil (CNBB), chaired by D. Evaristo Arns, Cardinal of Sao Paulo and member of the IFDA Council.

Those preliminary discussions, together with several meetings involving members of the IBASE team and representatives of popular organizations, stressed the urgent need for a systematic service of the kind proposed by IBASE. As a result of the support given to the project in the initial discussions, several workshops were organized to develop in detail IBASE's activity plans and to discuss forms of articulation with the popular movement. Leaders of trade-unions, grass-roots communities and others participated in those workshops.

The inputs received by the team permitted the completion of IBASE's program proposal by March 1980. The proposal took into account the needs of reliable data accumulation, information sharing and consultancy of the popular movement, as expressed in those workshops.

Implementation of the program

IBASE receives information and analysis demands of popular groups, and transmits them to appropriate working groups (composed mostly of technicians on a voluntary basis) constituted and coordinated by the IBASE team. The working group, together with the human and material resources of IBASE's data bank, gathers the required data and elaborates reports which are returned to the requesting groups for evaluation (is the information in the report satisfactory? Is the language of the analytical material adequate and understandable? Does the data require more elaboration? Does it agree with preliminary information already in the hands of the requesting popular groups? etc.).

The popular group will then be able to use the requested analytical report elaborated by IBASE as an input to formulate guidelines for action. As a result of such an interaction, a three-way learning process is established, as follows: (a) IBASE personnel and volunteer technicians learn about the real and most urgent information needs of the popular movement; (b) the popular group learns about data interpretation, reliable information sources, analytical methods, and so forth; (c) IBASE provides a link through which different popular organizations can share their knowledge and problems. The basis for a popular information-sharing network on a national scale is thus established.

A key element in implementing such an information-sharing linkage is the development of a suitable, effective, reliable and easily accessible data bank, so that source data can be processed and utilized in real-time and not simply as memory of the past. IBASE is designing the data bank with the help of popular leaders and volunteer technicians. In order to quickly process and output some key indicators, a small data processing system based on a personal-scale microcomputer has been installed and is fully operational. In addition, a reference library has been receiving information materials from many national and international sources.

An example of the way in which IBASE relates to the popular groups; in a meeting between IBASE's volunteer group of economists and leaders of shipbuilding workers' unions these leaders requested IBASE's help to gather information on the financial situation of shipyards; the unions were initiating the discussion of new contracts and had to confront the managers' argument that the companies were near bankruptcy and therefore significant wage increases were out of question. With the help of the data bank, updated information on the companies was immediately made available to the unions, and more reports are being prepared to help them organize their 1981 wage campaign.

Organization and availability of services

A project of this nature must of course establish limits within which it can provide effective services. Thus, for the purpose of organizing the data bank and of giving priority to the technical fields, which are of main interest to the needs of popular organizations, IBASE has framed its availability of services into four 'analytical modules' covering government policies: the economic structure; the social and political structure and international relations. These modules can be expanded and diversified whenever human and material resources allow it and upon specific requests. The modules serve only to define the technical fields within which IBASE is able to deliver consultancy and support services to the popular movement in their elaboration of alternative policy proposals; they are not 'research modules'.*

---

* Translated by *IFDA Dossier 30*, Nyon (Switzerland), July/August 1982.

Appendix 3. The Crisis of Software: Contribution to a Dossier

IBM: profiting from the weaknesses of others

Software is distressingly lacking. This is what justifies the approach of IBM-Colombia in searching for ways to develop software. Executives of data processing firms make no secret of this; it is a problem not only in Latin America, but throughout the world. All possible efforts are being mobilized to lay the foundations and stimulate the development of the software industry. In 1981, the worldwide policy of IBM went in three directions: it made a truce with independent software producers and will now recommend independently produced software to users; it has reached out to independent software vendors to develop software for new micro-, mini-, and personal computers; finally, it is encouraging its own employees to develop software packages by offering them a share of the profits (Snyders, 1981).

It is too soon to evaluate the fallout of this search for new partners in the Latin American social fabric. On the other hand, the experience of certain European countries, like Belgium, in the process of rapid computerization, gives food for thought. These examples should be seen as contributions to a dossier which has only just been opened.

Properly speaking, Belgium possesses no computer hardware industry or any related industry. As an official of the Ministry of Education noted: "In Belgium, when one buys a terminal for use in schools, money leaves the country . . . If it gave work to Belgian firms, the problem would be different. But all the hardware comes from other countries" (Authom, 1981). Belgium has not grasped the opportunity of extending its telematic network in the educational, banking, industrial, and telephonic fields by producing equipment within the country. From this point of view, countries like Cuba (with a very limited domestic market) and Brazil (with a very large domestic market), but also like India and

Singapore, have national computer policies much more developed than that of Belgium, a fact which should give certain industrialized countries something to think about.

One thing is certain in Belgium. The absence of an official industrial policy linked to the extension of telematic networks is consistent with the absence of a policy of institutional computer use. The case of education is the most revealing. In numerous sectors, there is growing concern over the possible repetition of the experience of introducing audiovisual equipment into schools, which, it is generally agreed, was a disaster, but did not result in critical evaluations, which would have been very useful when computers were beginning to be introduced into the educational system.

Everything points to the fact that, for the moment, developments are moving in the same direction. In a symposium organized by trade unions on the impact of telematics in 1981, one could read: "Faced with the present vacuum, the Commission insists on the role of the public authorities, as much in the training of teachers in the perspective of a balanced approach to computers, as in the development of an adapted pedagogy. If this is not done, education will become the victim of the commercial designs of computer firms" (Groupement national des cadres-CSC, 1981).

In the absence of an overall policy of planning for possible methods for software production, it is difficult to evaluate the private initiatives which, under the patronage of the big computer firms, have attempted to occupy a field that, here to fore has been neglected. The way in which IBM has succeeded in penetrating the Belgian educational system, in order to stimulate the formation of social uses for computers, should be analyzed in terms of the shortcomings of the public authorities.

The goal of this program, EIE (*Enseignement-Informatique-Entreprise*), initiated at the beginning of 1980 is to teach secondary pupils the basic principles of computers and their use in professional life, by permitting them to use small 5,120 computers. This project is placed within the framework of a close cooperation between business and teaching. Participants include about 20 colleges or schools, for the most part private, and about 30 industrial organizations, ranging from the local concessionary of Coca-Cola to Cyanamid Benelux, as well as numerous local firms. All of these firms have helped the schools install teaching equipment by proposing programs of practical training through conferences and demonstrations based on real applications and even practical work within the firms themselves. As the directors of IBM pointed out: "This direct exchange between the practitioners of the enterprise and pupils is one of the best possible means of education, as much for the effective experience of computer management as the realistic introduction to the real life of the enterprise. . . . As for IBM, it has contributed to the development of the project by organizing courses for the teachers of the schools taking part and by assuring the coordination and the exchange of programs between schools" (IBM-Brussels, 1981). Beyond these activities, centered on the industrial-school exchange, work groups have studied the use of the computer in three areas: the administrative management of the school; the teaching of information science; and computer-assisted teaching in mathematics, physics, chemistry, history, and languages.

Social counter-scenarios

Beyond this limited experiment the introduction of a firm like IBM into the education system, whether public or private, illustrates the new strategies adopted by large hardware firms to promote the creation of software. "We must promote intellectual development and spread knowledge. We must develop the software we lack. Private firms cannot do it, but teachers familiar with the school and pedagogical methods ought to develop programs. Small countries like Belgium have no other solution than to recycle their active population into informatics" argued an IBM manager when presenting the experiment at a recent symposium on the cultural industries in Brussels (Dawans, 1982). By arguing thus, without knowing it, perhaps, he posed an essential question: what will be the place of a little industrialized country such as Belgium in the new international division of labor? He revealed, in passing, that from now on, in the search for social uses for the new microelectronic products, it is necessary to proceed by a "decentralization of discourse," permitting those who have never been able to express themselves to speak through the invention of programs. A new schema of relations between industry and civil society is proposed. This proposal has all the more chance of being accepted if there is no national computerization policy, constructed on another schema of relations between different social actors. Such a policy was demanded recently, by trade unions: "This information and training should allow (social actors) to react critically to this flow of data. The public authorities, teachers, consumers' associations and unions should be the instruments responsible for this training" (Groupement national des cadres-CSC, 1981, p. 83).

It is a counter-scenario of this type which is proposed by initiatives like that of the Galileo Centre of the University of Louvain-la-Neuve, which is stimulating thinking on microcomputer experiments in workers' groups, non-profit groups, and cooperatives, thus posing the problem of the appropriation of computers by different social categories. An informatics which acts against an exaggerated centralization and individualization would be the base of a network of small management, accounting, and documentation groups at the service of associations and trade unions. By posing questions on the possible actors and how they can organize themselves, groups like these propose principles of what could be a response to the implicit models of computerization of everyday life proposed by the new private cultural prospectors.

> The example of nuclear power shows that once a structure is installed, it is difficult to influence it, even when it does not respond to a social demand. So, what is to be done? Concretely analyze the organization of resources in terms of their real utility, by taking into account their impact on different situations (health, inequalities, access to these resources, needs, etc.).
> Reflect, of course,. But above all, act quickly. Where are the actors? How is it possible to organize? 1. An ostrich-like policy is pointless. First, everyone—animator, health worker, trade union militant—must use these machines and become informed. Then they can demand the right to information and speaking facilities and remain in control without fear of their relative incompetence. 2) Training exists. But it is important to be attentive to its role and content. In effect, a certain form of training implicitly underlies a certain type of computerization scenario. 3) The demand must intervene from the conception of the process; if not, it can no longer be stopped. It is therefore important to negotiate, from this stage on, by participating in research, pilot projects, and experiments. 4) Some options already exist and call for precise positions on the part of trade unions and various associations. An example is the introduction of computers in or through the public sector. Room for dialogue exists that must be used and transformed into efficient means of exercizing pressure on decisions. 5) Such action requires alliances between the various interested groups. For a trade union, this means increasing attention to the problems that affect everyday life. (Groupement national des cadres-CSC, 1981, pp. 75–79)

These lines of action are even more important when one considers that day after day throughout Europe the role assumed by big transnational corporations of promoter of social uses for the new technologies is being confirmed.

The privatization of teaching?

If it is certain that there is never enough concern shown in time to thwart a certain model of the computerization of everyday life within the associative movement, it is also certain that one of the principal terrains where the relation between transnational firms, computerization and civil society is played out is currently in the field of computer-aided learning in countries such as Belgium. The public authorities do not seem to be playing the dynamic role that some expected of the Ministry of National Education. "It is abnormal that computer aided learning should be due to isolated, private initiatives, which can, voluntarily or not, increase the risks and inconveniences" (Groupement national des Cadres-CSC, 1982, p. 83).

Since August 1980, the Plato system (from Control Data) has been in operation at the Free University of Brussels. This was the first Plato system sold outside the United States and Canada. In 1975, Control Data attempted to sell its system to Venezuela, but without success. Teaching circles saw in this initiative the threat of colonization and succeeded in stopping negotiations already well underway (Sutz, 1982, pp. 11–12). In one year, the Free University of Brussels has developed about 50 hours of original courses over and above those it translated and adapted from the United States. The objective aimed at for the moment is the passage from high school to university. The advantages of the Plato system are the length of experience with the system and the access to the library of programs perfected in the U.S., which comprise more than 8,000 hours of courses in subjects ranging from chemistry to languages and economics. Its disadvantage is the necessity for giving the content of the courses to a computer scientist for programing.

Another system (DOCEO), developed in Belgium by the Faculty of Applied Sciences at the University of Liège, is also in the running. Inaugurated more than 16 years ago and after use in medical applications (collecting and organizing medical information, patients' histories, and medical teaching programs), the DOCEO system offers an audiovisual supplement, commanded by the computer program, used in addition to the keyboard and its terminal. This combination of sound-image-computer gives it an advantage over the Plato system. Its extremely simplified language comprises no more than a dozen instructions. It can be learned in two or three hours. Thus, teacher can create a course without recourse to a computer scientist. The problem for the creators of DOCEO is to find an alliance with private or public industry which could manufacture the equipment. The problem for the operators of the Plato system lies elsewhere: "If we can perfect courses, we could be very competitive on a world scale for the French language" (*Pourquoi Pas?*, 1981a). Here, we have two conceptions of a policy for very different purposes. The objective of the creators of DOCEO is that every teacher can understand the language of the machine and participate in the development of courses without prior computer knowledge. "It is", they say, "a question of democratic pedagogy" (*Pourquoi Pas?*, 1981b). The supporters of Plato do not seem to be at all concerned by this problem. They are seeking, leaning on the immense reserves accumulated by Control Data, to offer translated programs and to add their own.

As, in the case of audiovisual programs, the conclusive argument,

which consists in affirming that the "accumulated reserves" of big data
processing firms command the margin of elasticity within which alter-
natives are to be debated, is making inroads in the area of new information and communications technologies. "We have already ordered from
the United States, which has accumulated a lot of programs, a dozen
programs available, to see how they could fit into our experiment, and
then we will make exchanges," stated the director of IBM's EIE experiment, trying to "naturalize" this cooperation, discrediting in advance any
questioning of an exchange marked by an unequal relation of forces.

But that is not all. One leitmotiv runs through the statements of the
IBM project operators: the need to arrive at a standard project, a standardized configuration of the computer which allows the free flow of
information between enterprise and school. "The material chosen, widespread in numerous industries, functions, and professions, allows the
easy exchange of information and programs either by means of the
floppy disk which is sent through the post, or processing over distance,
the computer in this case being used as an intelligent terminal" (IBM-
Brussels, 1981). The perfection of a standard software which allows for
an interchangeable library of programs, standard training, and standard
management, the constitution of small banks of standard data which will
help children prepare their work and avoid having them carry out long
personal research is what is in store, if the IBM project is carried through
to its logical conclusion. The normal procedure will result, at the end of a
project in an appeal to the hegemonic program bank when local production is lacking or too expensive (it is estimated that from 60 to 400 hours
are needed to manufacture a program for one hour of courses). The
fluidity of information between enterprise and school thus becomes the
first condition of this universal exchange of knowledge and know-how.
The computer, situated in this new balance of power, projects the educational apparatus into the reference universe of transnational thinking.
Seen in this perspective, decentralization in the manufacturing of software runs the risk of metamorphizing into a sham participation. The local
mobilization of teachers and pupils for the conception of programs is
important only in inducing demand for an existing stock of programs and
above all for the modeling of what the Japanese already call "the infor-
matic mentality." The latter, in the view of transnational firms, sweeps
aside all specificities and diversities in so far as they are dissidences and
only integrates them into the schema of decentralized production if these
local particularities become exchangeable currency and the passport of
the world citizen, in short, only if they reproduce the legitimacy of their
particular conception of the universal by means of the standardization
process.

One would, however, cut short an accusation, which turns out to be more complex than simply considering the case of Belgium, in the face of new information technologies applied to the education field, by limiting it to projects like that of IBM. The latter are not widespread in Europe, where most states are increasingly wary of the alliance between the school and the transnational firm. Other pressures are at work in this area. Little known as they are, local or community television experiments are one of the alternative pressures that reposition education and training in a more democratic debate than that of the IBM experiment.

Some of these television experiments signify a new articulation between trade unions and social movements, training and community media. Other less well-known and more disseminated experiments are also moving towards a rearticulation of the relation between community media and the school. This tends to be demonstrated in very embryonic fashion by the work begun in several schools where developers of community televisions have set in motion a process of video socialization in the school environment. Extremely heterogeneous in their orientation, and above all in their results, these few efforts, as yet uncontrolled, testify to the search for a pedagogy in which decentralization and the return to the local are at the center of research into what is implied by participation as a new mode of exchange between teachers and pupils, schools and local communities. Production is varied; short local televised programs on a local person or problem, playlets on racism, etc., serve as links between the various community television programs, by redefining the school-society relation in the sense of a breaking out of the school framework into the neighbourhood and the town, transformed into a place of investigation, contact, and research. Whereas the IBM experiment cuts short the long process of research by making small standardized data banks available to children, these other projects go in the opposite direction and rediscover the process of investigation as a process of social apprenticeship and the creation of relations between different people, groups, and circles.

References

AEC. (Asociacão dos empregados de Cobra). (1981). *COBRA: a visão da AEC.* (May). Rio de Janeiro. Mimeographed.

Alvarado, M. C. (1980). "Pondrían satélite colombiano en órbita geostacionaria." *El Espectador,* Bogota, (August 22).

Arjian, R. (1979). "Brazil links Communications with Tomorrow." *Telecommunications,* (April).

Arveras, J. (1981). "Un cable para tener imagen y color." *Clarin,* Buenos Aires, (May 5).

Arvonny, M. (1981). "Du micro à l'ordinateur individuel." *Le Monde,* Paris (September 25), 25.

Asociación colombiana de usuarios de computadoras (1980). *Noticias.* (March–April).

Authom, P. (1981). Interview with M. Deladrière, in report on "L'ordinateur a l'école." *Pourquoi Pas?,* Brussels, (October 29), 68–76.

Barquin, R., et al. (1976). "A Model for Progress in Developing Nations." *Datamation,* (September), 190A–190H.

Bennaceur, S. and Gèze, F. (1980). "New forms of technological Dependence in Developing Countries inherent in the Worldwide Organization of the Electronics Industry." *In* D. Ernst (Ed.), *The New International Division of Labour, Technology, and Under-Development.* 255–280. Frankfurt/New York: Campus Verlag.

Blair, J. (1981). "Technology Transfer via Satellite." *Revista Nacional de Telecomunicações.* Sao Paolo, (March).

Brazilian Association of Professional Data Processing. (1981). *2nd Congresso Nacional de profissionais de processamento de dados.* Commission 2: National Computer Policy. Curitiba, (June 18–21).

Brazilian Parliament. (1979). *Elementos para o debate de implantaçao de serviço de cabodifusão no Brasil.* Presented by C. Valente, L. Lansetta, and D. Herz. (September).

Brigagão, C. (1981). "Le cas du Brésil: forteresse ou rideau de papier." *Impact: Science et Société 31,* (1).

Business Week. (1979). "A Warm Climate for Electronics." (August 20).

Business Week. (1980). "Citibank: a rising giant in computer services." (August 4), 54–56.

Business Week. (1981a). "A Latin Telecommunications Boom." (May 25), 168.

Business Week. (1981b). "Colombia: the Jockeying to Build the First Latin Satellite." (August 24), 45.

Business Week. (1981c). "Brazil: A Frustrated ITT Quits a Hot Market." (November 2).

Business Week. (1982). "Asia: Automation is Hitting a Low-Wage Bastion." International Edition, (March 15), 29–32.

Castaneda, J. (1982). "Mexique: une crise économique aggravée par la rigidité du système politique." *Le Monde Diplomatique,* (October), 13.

Castro Caycedo, G. (1981). *El libro blanco de la TV.* Bogota: Editorial Hispana.

Chabreuil, A. (1980). "Les satellites d'observation de la terre." *Futuribles.* (Paris), (November), 27.

Chamoux, J. P. (1980). *Information sans frontières.* Paris: La Documentation française.

Clarin. (1981). "Informática latino-americana." Buenos Aires, (March 31), 4.

Communicación y Cultura. (1975). Dossier published by the journal Communicación y Cultura. Buenos Aires–Mexico City, No. 3.

Contraloria general de la Republica. (1980). *El Teleproceso, un sistema revolucionario.* Panama.

Crozier, M., Huntington, S., and Watanuki, J. (1975). *The Crisis of Democracy.* New York: New York University Press.

Cuban Delegation. (1980). *Educación en informática en la Republica de Cuba.* Document presented by Cuban delegation to the first meeting on informatics in Caracas.

Da Costa Marques, I. (1975). "O momento decisivo para o computador brasileiro." *Dados e Ideias,* Rio de Janeiro, (August–September), 14–15.

Da Costa Marques, I. (1975–1976). "Uma necessidade vital." *Dados e Ideias.* Rio de Janeiro, (December 1975–January 1976), 10.

Datamation. (1980). "Going Global." (September), 138.

Datamation. (1981a). "Software Success Story." (May).

Datamation. (1981b). "Tracking Europe's Top 25." (November), 37.

Datamation. (1981c). Special Report. (December).

Dawans, M. (1982). Address of M. Dawans. *In Actes des Rencontres "Industries Culturelles",* Brussels, 159–161.

de Cindio, F., and de Michelis, C. (Eds.) (1980). *Il progetto Cybersyn: cibernetica per la democrazia.* Milan: CLUP-CLUED.

de la Cruz, R. (1981). "Développement, État, et division du travail: contribution à la critique de la technologie capitaliste." Unpublished doctoral thesis, (May). Universite de Paris VIII–Paris X, Paris.

Delapierre, M., and Zimmerman, J. B. (1983). "Le tiers monde et l'informatique: de la technique aux choix politiques." *Amérique Latine,* Paris, (January–February), 36.

de Rose, F. (1978). "Les progrès scientifiques et techniques: les problèmes qu'ils posent à l'ouest." *Revue de l'OTAN,* Brussels, (October), 20.

de Souza Costa Barros, A. (1980). *Dissemination and Use of Social Sciences Research among and by Policy Makers.* Unpublished survey for the Tinker Foundation, Brazilia (Brazil).

Emmanuel, A. (1981). *Technologie appropriée ou technologie sous-développée.* Paris: PUF–IRM.

Ernst, D. (1983). *The Global Race in Microelectronics. Innovation and Corporate Strategies in a Period of Crisis.* Frankfurt am Main/New York: Campus.

FAST. Research Team of European Communities. (1982). *Le potentiel de création d'emplois des technologies de l'information.* Research report. (February). Brussels.

Festinger, G. and Joxe, D. (1981). "L'absence du secteur associatif." *Le Monde,* (September 30), 19.

Final Report. Survey of Venezuelan Market for Computers and Related Equipment. (1980). Unpublished report for U.S. Department of Commerce. (December).

Flichy, P. (1980). *Les industries de l'imaginaire.* Grenoble: Presses universitaires de Grenoble.

Flores Salgado, J., and Conde Luna, L. (1979). *Televisión por cable otro factor de integración regional de Mexico.* (July). Mexico City: Ticom, Universidad Autonoma Metropolitana de Mexico.

Fondation A. L. 2001. (1978). *Comunicación y comunidad científica en Colombia.* Bogota. (Unpublished).

Fröbel, F., Heinrichs, J., and Kreye, O. (1980). *The New International Division of Labor.* Cambridge University Press.

Frundt. H. J. (1980). *Objecciones de accionistas cristianos contra la Gulf & Western.* Santo Domingo: Publicaciones Estudios Sociales.

Futuribles. (1980). "Forum: La specialisation industrielle en Europe." (October), 73–82.

Garcia Castro, F. (1980). "Las responsabilidades de ser el hermano mayor." *Informatica,* Santiago de Chile, (September), 14–18.

Gardner, W. D. (1981). "Mexico's Move to Micros." *Datamation,* (June), 192–14.

Gennari Netto, O. (1981). "A sociedade pós-industrial." *Boletin Informativo.* Secretaria Especial de Informatica, Brasilia. (1), (March–April), 50–51.

Giordani, G. (1976). *Análisis de la indústria electrónica y de telecommunicaciones en Venezuela.* Caracas: CENDES, Universidad central de Venezuela. Mimeographed.

Gonzalez-Manet, E. (1981). *Politica cultural y medios de difusión masiva en Cuba.* Unpublished paper. Havana.

Groupement national des cadres-CSC. (1981). *Journées de l'informatique et de la télématique.* Brussels, November 21–22.

Guedes Batelho, T. M. (1976). "A informação disponivel em sistemas no Brasil." *Dados e Ideias.* Rio de Janeiro, (June–July), 61.

Higher School of War. (1978). *Aspectos da doutrina da Escola superior de guerra e de suas bases teoricas.* Brazil. Mimeographed.

Hoffman, K., and Rush, H. (1980). "Micro-electronics, Industry, and the Third World." *Futures,* (August).

Ho Kwon Ping. (1981). "Bargaining on the Free Trade Zones." *Far Eastern Economic Review,* 12.

IBI/QUA. (1982). *La circulation des données en Afrique.* Rome: IBI/QUA SPO2.

IBM-Brussels. (1981). *Enseignement-Informatique-Entreprise.* Presentation of the project. Brussels: IBM-Brussels.

Informática. (1979a). "IBM, bastante mas que computación." Santiago de Chile, (April), 16–19.

Informática. (1979b). "Desarrollo de la utilización de la tecnologia de computadoras en Chile." Santiago de Chile, (May).

Jaramillo, C. E. (1979). "Stratégie pour l'introduction en Colombie de la technologie éducative." *Revue Tiers-Monde XX,* (79), Paris, PUF, (July–September).

Junta de administración y vigilancia. (1981). *Zona franca de Iquique: objetivos, desarrollo y perspecitvas.* (March), Chile. Mimeographed.

La Tercera de la Hora. (1981). "Quién tiene la información tiene también el poder." (Conversation with the President of ECOM). (September 27), 10.

Le Monde Diplomatique. (1980). "Réseaux sans frontières." Dossier on international networks. Paris, (December).

Le Nouvel Observateur. (1982). "Informatique: comment la France invente le nouveau cerveau du monde." Conversation with J. J. Servan-Schrieber. (June 5), 65.

Lindeborg, L. (1982). *L'informatique en Suède.* Stockholm: Svenska Institute.

Lloyd, A. and Peltu, M. (1981). "The Power of the PTT." *Datamation,* (March), 216–218.

McAnany, E., and Oliviera, J. B. (1980). *The SACI/EXERN Project in Brazil: An Analytical Case Study.* UNESCO.

McCarter, P. M. (1980). "Report on Transborder Data-Flow Policies." *Computer Decisions,* (September), 93.

Madec, A. (1982). *Les flux transfrontières de données.* Paris: La Documentation française.

Martin Barbero, J. (1982). "De quelques defis pour la recherche sur la communication en Amérique Latine." *Amérique Latine,* Paris, (January–March), 43–48.

Mattelart, A. (1979a, 1983). "Introduction." *In* A. Mattelart and S. Siegelaub (Eds.), *Communication and Class Struggle, an anthology.* Vol. 1 and Vol. 2. New York: International General.

Mattelart A. (1979b). *Multinational Corporations and the Control of Culture.* Brighton: Harvester, and Atlantic Highlands, NJ: Humanities Press.

Mattelart, A. (1979c). "The Ideology of the Military State." *In* A. Mattelart and S. Siegelaub (Eds.), *Communication and Class Struggle,* Vol. 1, 402–427. New York: International General.

Mattelart, A. (1983). *Transnationals and the Third World: The Struggle for Culture.* MA: Bergin and Garvey.

Mattelart, A. and M. (1979). *De l'usage des médias en temps de crise.* Paris: Ed. Alain Moreau.

Mattelart A., and Stourdzé, Y. (1982). *Technologie, Culture et Communication.* Paris: La Documentation française. (Published in English under the title *Technology, Culture and Communication in France: a Report to the Minister of Research and Industry* (1985). Amsterdam (Netherlands)—New York: North-Holland Publishing.

Mercado. (1981). "Informática: el futuro ya es presente." Buenos Aires, (March 5).

Mexico. Secretaria de programación y presupuesto. (1980). *Politica informática gubernamental.* Mexico City.

Mexico. Secretaria de programación y presupuesto. (1981). *Diagnostico de la informatica en Mexico 1980.* Mexico City.

Michalet, C. A. (1982). Report on South Korea. In *Le Monde,* Paris, (October 9).

Millan, H. R., and Hermes de Araujo, J. L. (1979). "Na palabra dos técnicos um ponto de vista nacional." *Cadernos de tecnologia e ciéncia.* Rio de Janeiro, (December–January 1979), 29–40.

Mirow, K. (1978). *A ditadura dos carteis.* Rio de Janeiro: Civilizacao Brasiliera.

Mitterrand, President F. (1982). *Technologie, emploi, et croissance.* Report of President Mitterrand to the summit of industrialized countries, Château de Versailles, (June 5).

Moreno Fraginals, M. (1978). *El ingenio, complejo economico social cubano del azucar.* Vol. 3. Havana: Editorial de Ciencias Sociales.

Movimiento Antonio José de Sucre. (1976). *Boletin 1,* (1). Caracas.

Nadel, L. and Wiener, H. (1977). "Would You Sell a Computer to Hitler." *Computer Decisions.* (February).

North American Congress on Latin America. (NACLA). (1975). "Hit and Run. US Runaway shops on the Mexican Border." Report in *NACLA's Latin America and Empire Report.* (July–August).

North American Congress on Latin America. (NACLA). (1977). "Electronics: the Global Industry." *NACLA's Latin America and Empire Report.* (April).

Parente, E. (1979). "O desafio da informação." *Revista Nacional de Telecomunicações.* Sao Paolo, Brazil, (May), 72.

Pastré, O. (1982). "Informatisation et emploi: des mythes a la réalité." *Culture Technique 7,* (March). Paris.

Pastré, O., et al. (1981). *Informatisation et emploi: menace ou mutation.* Paris: La Documentation française.

Perrouin, L. (1982). "Le Venezuela, terre d'avenir." *Revue Française des Télécommunications,* Paris, (July).

Philips. (1980). *Annual Report,* 1980 Eindhoven. Netherlands.

Pino, J. A. (1980). "Nivel nacional de desarrollo de la computación." *Informatica,* Santiago, Chile, (July), 17.

Pourquoi Pas? (1981a). Interview with Professor Beaufrays in the feature "L'ordinateur a l'ecole." Brussels, (November 5), 68–69.

Pourquoi Pas? (1981b). Interview with M. Leclercq, assistant to Professor de Landsheere, director of the laboratory of experimental pedagogy of Sart Tilman, Liege. Brussels, (November 5), 70–71.

Rada, J. (1981a). "The Microelectronics Revolution: Implications for the Third World." *Development Dialogue 2.* Uppsala, Sweden. 41–67.

Rada, J. (1981b). *Microelectronics, Information Technology and its Effects on Developing Countries.* Geneva: ILO.

Revista Nacional de Telecomunicações. (1980a). "1962: na lei, a arrancada que viria tres anos depois." São Paolo, (September), 19–30.

Revista Nacional de Telecomunicações. (1980b). "Haroldo defende a privatização." São Paolo, (September), 81.

Salinas, R. (1979). *Televisión chilena: la opción del color.* Unpublished typed report, UNESCO-ILET contract, Santiago, Chile.

Schiller, H. (1981). *Who Knows: Information in the Age of the Fortune 500.* Norwood, NJ: Ablex Publishing.

Secretaria Especial de Informatica. (SEI). (1981). "Recursos computacionais brasileiros." *Boletin Informativo,* Brazilia, (January–February.)

Secretaria Especial de Informatica. (SEI). (1982). *Boletin Informativo.* (January– March). Brazilia, Brazil: SEI.

SER/IBM (Colombia). (n.d.). *Laboratorio inter-institucional de sistemas. (LIS).* Bogota.

Servan-Schreiber, J. J. (1980). *Le défi mondial.* Paris: Fayard.

Siqueira, E. (1979). "Violação da privacidade, o crime impune." *O Estado de São Paolo.* (July 8), 24.

Snyders, J. (1981). "What's coming down the pike in software." *Computer Decisions,* (September), 122–142.

Souza, M. (1980). "No sufoco da zona." *Folha de São Paolo.* (April 13), 5.

S. Prenafeta J. (1980). "Registro civil e identificación: renovarse o morir." *Informática,* Santiago du Chile, (May), 14.

Sutz, J. (1982). *La ofensiva telemática.* (Paper). Caracas: CENDES.

Thery, G. (1982). "Prendre la mesure du défi électronique." *Le Monde,* (September 22), 33.

Time Inc. (1981). *Home Video: A Global Report.* Report presented to ITA European Home Video Seminar, Cannes, France, (October 11). Unpublished.

Tirado, G. (1980). *Análisis y perspectivas de la indústria, maquinarias aparatos, equipos y materiales eléctricos y electrónicos (1971–1978).* Caracas, CENDES, Universidad central de Venezuela. Mimeographed.

Toffler, A. (1980). *The Third Wave.* New York: William Morrow.

TV Globo. (1980). *Rede Globo, 15 anos.* Brazil.

United Nations Center on Transnational Corporations. (1982). *Transnational Corporations and Transborder Data Flows: A Technical Paper.* New York: UN.

U.S. Department of Commerce. (1976). *Brazil: Overseas Business Reports.* Washington, D.C.: GPO.

U.S. Senate (1971). "US Policies and Programs in Brazil." *Hearings Before the Subcommittee on Western Hemisphere Affairs.* (May 4–5, 11). Washington DC: US Senate.

Yarce, J. (1980). "TV publica o TV privada." *El Mundo,* Bogota, (August 19).

Author Index

Italics indicate bibliographic citations.

Subject Index

S

Saci-Exern, 57

Satellites, 53, 57–59, 80, 127–130, 142

Security, 36–37, 57–58 (*see also* National security)

SEI (Brazilian Special Secretariat for Informatics), 110–111

SER (Interdisciplinary center of independent professionals), 91–92, 139–140 (*see also* IBM)

SERLA Project, 57

SERPRO (Federal data processing service, Brazil), 104–106, 112

Siemens, 61, 63

Silicon Valley, 111

SITA (Société internationale pour la télécommunication aéronautique), 121

Sony (*see* Japanese firms)

Smuggling networks (*see* Videocassettes)

Spar Aerospace, 58–59

Swift, 80–83, 121, 130

Sycor, 107

Sylvania, 19

Systems Development Corp., 90, 122–123

Systems theory, 87, 92

T

Tandy, 76

Technicians, professionals, specialists: and computer policy, 111–112; lack of 91–92; lack of studies on, 113–114; and research, 5, 154–155; and search for software, 131–133; and social movements, 139–142, 151–152; and State, 112, 114–115 (*see also* Popular control on information)

Telebras, 102–103, 145

Telecommunications institutions, 5, 54 n.4, 64, 76, 101–103

Telenet, 87, 97, 123

Telephones, 6–7, 59–64, 103, 146

Teletext, 90

Televisa (Mexico), 49–50

Televisa Foundation, 50–52

Telidon (*see* Teletext)

Television, 10, 17–19, 34, 43–56, 102, 172

Telrad Telecommunications, 62

Thomson-CSF (*see* French firms)

Thyssen Group, 125

Tiros-N (*see* NOAA)

Torrijos–Carter agreements, 28

Torrijos, Omar (General), 87

Transborder data flows (TDF), 1–2, 6, 10–11, 82, 121–126, 130–135, 149

Transfer of technology: and consumer electronics industry, 18–19; and free trade zones, 24–25, 30–31; and industrial strategy, 95, 104–110, 133–135; and model of consumption, 71; and new systems of data processing, 44–45; and North/South relations, 153–155; and security strategy, 11–12; and software, 132, 170–171; and telephonic infrastructure, 60–61

Transnationals: Asian transnationals, 25; and consumer electronics industry, 17–20; and educational software, 167–172; and European markets, 75–77; and free trade zones, 20–32; and information industry, 122–126; regulation on, 133–135; and relocalization, 3 (*see also* French firms, Japanese firms, Philips, etc.)

Trilateral Commission, 113–114

Trinidad & Tobago (free trade zones), 22, 32

Trumbo, Dalton, 13

Tymnet, 123

U

Unequal development of State, 90

UNESCO, 133, 149

United Brands (TRT Telecommunications), 71

Universities: and cable TV, 52 n.3; crisis of the university system, 91; and critical research, 154–155, 168–169; and IBM, 137–139; and national computers industries, 104 n.5, 106, 111; and privatization, 169–172; and satellites, 57; and television networks, 43, 50

UNIDO (United Nations Industrial Development Organization), 30

Univac, 137

USAID (Agency of International Development), 117, 141

US Commerce Department, 18, 46, 67

Uruguay: computers development, 69;